AF587732

Once more, it's a journey to the fringes. Recalling resistant and peculiar aesthetics, wondrous and forgotten outgrowths of music and cultural history of the last seventy years – a search for works with inherent value, often contrary to a semblance of seriosity. The essays and portraits deal with liminal figures, with failed, half-successful projects, with experiences of rupture and transitory states, with unconscious processes and hidden atmospheres – with the edges of the self, of one's reason and beyond. Based on artists and groups such as French-Iranian cohort Vox Populi!, Japanese director Takahisa Zeze, visual artist and poet Unica Zürn or German writer Wolfgang Hilbig, the contributors try to make these facets visible with narrative potency, without neglecting their own inclinations and idiosyncrasies. And since it has always been *Lärm*'s declared aim to pursue a more subjective, less didactic approach, there is also a prose text to be found at the end of this issue.

LÄRM FANZINE

Second Issue

Essays

Lärm Publications
Berlin
2021

Layout: Benedikt Eiden
Printing and Binding: Königsdruck GmbH, Berlin
Paper: Munken Pure Rough 100 g/m^2, PEYDUR 270 g/m^2
Typeface: LTC Bodoni, Studio Pro

ISBN 978-3-00-070392-8

info@laerm-publications.com

CONTENTS

It was a day in our near future ...

Hands of steel, 1986

HUNTERS OF FUTURE PAST

Visions from the 1980s Italian post-atomic b-movie extravaganza

---

by Valeria Calderoni

I'm broadcasting live from one of those moody altered states of consciousness some of us love to navigate, sliding among dreamlike mindscapes and ghastly worst-case scenarios as we search for the meaning of reality. We might not agree on what defines it, but we have become aware that the plane of existence we inhabit shares an increasing amount of features with the bleakest versions of the future imagined by our dystopian literature and movies, which goes to explain the newfound popularity of the genre these days. I make no exception, as many of the movies I gravitated towards during the past year are concerned with the depiction of life in the aftermath of man-made disaster.

Half hidden behind the well-deserved glory of films considered of greater cultural value, of which they recreate the themes, the atmospheres and the aesthetic, lies the particular subgenre I've been diving into lately: the 1980s wave of post-apocalyptic b-movies directed by Italian masters of genre cinema such as Lucio Fulci, Enzo G. Castellari, Sergio Martino and Joe D'Amato – films mostly commissioned to them to capitalize on the international success of *Mad Max*, *Escape From New York* and *The Warriors*.

A Sucker For B-Movies

I admit to being a sucker for B, C and even some Z movies since I was a teenager. I remember some blissful afternoons of late summer and early fall, in the first lazy weeks of school, riding the scooter to meet my friends at the video store and renting as many movies as we could possibly binge watch on a weekend. Obviously we were never too much into open air activities and spent most of our time in dusty basements and rehearsal spaces blasting with music, wrapped in a thick cloud of smoke – the ideal nurturing ground for ever faithful b-movie aficionados.

With my adolescence set in the 'glory' days of Napster and dial-up internet access, the only b-movies I could access at the time were those included in my dad's selection of Roger Corman's timeless masterworks from the 1960s, like *The Man With The X-Ray Eyes* or his legendary gothic-horror eight-move Poe Cycle with Vincent Price, alongside some late night TV staples such as Lucio Fulci's *L'Aldilà* or Ciccio Ingrassia's *The Exorcist: Italian Style*. Then one evening, on the way home from the public library, I entered what is probably the smallest video rental store I've seen to this day. It was maybe lacking on some of the classics that could have made it more frequented, but the manager knew his Ted V. Mikels and his Russ Meyer and had stocked up on all sorts of b-movie treasures. I unexpectedly and suddenly got access to all of the stuff I'd only seen mentioned before in short but enthusiastic blurbs on the heavy metal magazines I used to read after school. Movies coming from the darkest, goofiest blind corners of the mind; failed or half-successful, yet always brave, attempts to recreate dreams and nightmares. The excitement and sense of wonder I felt when a film managed to work its magic despite – or actually even thanks to – the low-budget and DIY approach made me understand why some of my favorite bands had chosen to dedicate their best songs, if not their entire artistic output, to expressing their love for b-movies, especially those of the science fiction horror kind.

Some of those movies turned out to be less exciting than their bombastic titles had led me to believe, but on other occasions they managed to live up to the outlandish names and alluring trailers accompanying them. That magic often happened when visionary creators turned the camp control knob up to eleven without any shame or second thoughts – a line of business in which Troma Entertainment has been particularly successful – or when they managed to "mix exploitation film with art film... and make money", like John Waters said of Roger Corman before introducing him as one of his all time heroes at the Provincetown Film Festival in 2012. That's a lesson many directors learned from the "B-Movie King" himself – from his well-known apprentices like Francis Ford Coppola and Joe Dante to his overseas admirers like Enzo G. Castellari and Antonio Margheriti and other prolific genre-shifting directors.

The Apocalypse: Italian Style

If b-movies in general are somehow a fitting metaphor for life – with their poorly acted scenes and clumsy non sequiturs, alongside flashes of over-the-top genius and glory – then post-apocalyptic b-movies are well suited to the moods and fears of our times, as they portray life in the aftermath of man-made disaster caused by greediness and fear and exacerbated by racism and violence. Their Italian 1980s "post-atomic" division is part of an international trend launched by Miller and Carpenter and fueled by plenty of American, French, Japanese and even Filipino productions trying to imitate their formula, yet and it brought us some interesting portrayals of the future of our species.

I had a lucky chance to talk about this with Claudio Simonetti of Goblin, the man behind some of the most memorable soundtracks in the genre, thanks to my friend Andrea who passed him over to me on the phone. When I asked him which of his compositions would be best suited to our own apocalyptic times, Claudio said he'd choose the theme he wrote with Goblin for George Romero's *Dawn Of The Dead*, but agreed the one he made for Sergio Martino's *Hands of Steel* would be a good fit as well. Working on the soundtrack for Castellari's *The New Barbarians* as well as Martino's *Hands of Steel* allowed him to explore places in music he wouldn't have gone otherwise, he added. Since he usually works on the finished movie, Sergio Martino's dark vision of the future for *Hands of Steel* influenced him greatly in his work on the soundtrack. The movie turned out to be somehow prescient of our present and future, Claudio said, "because the worst is yet to come".

In fact, only some of the Italian so-called "post-atomic" movies are set in the aftermath of a nuclear holocaust. In the last years of the Cold War, nuclear warfare didn't seem like the only possible worst case scenario for mankind anymore. The 1980s were also "the decade we almost stopped climate change" according to *The New York Times*: Sergio Martino's 1986 movie *Hands Of Steel* argued that, if big corporations could have created an invincible cyborg to kill scientists who threatened to warn the authorities about the alarming levels of pollution caused by their business, they definitely would have – but they didn't need to, because the scientists who predicted the impact of fossil fuels on the environment already worked for them, as we now know. Lucio Fulci made a wager on the concept of eternal recurrence with *Warriors Of The Year 2072*, portraying a new authoritarian age in Rome where violent TV programs are used to pacify and distract the population from the harsh living conditions they endure. Gladiators on motorbikes evocative of George Romero's *Knightriders* ride in formation along Ponte Sant'Angelo in Rome, speeding towards their televised death match in a visually compelling representation of mankind's race towards its own destruction.

Enzo G. Castellari, known outside of Italy mostly for being one of Quentin Tarantino's favorite directors, contributed generously to the genre with no less than three movies. Taking the themes of *Mad Max* and *The Warriors* a few steps further into "bikexploitation" territory with *1990:The Bronx Warriors* and *The New Barbarians*, he ultimately put humanity's survival in the hands of rebel biker gangs, sometimes looking like the Hells Angels, other times more like cyberpunk templars of the future. The last and best of his triptych, *Escape From The Bronx*, envisions the dismal, darkest developments of unregulated gentrification in New York: a ruthless corporation employs a battalion of "disinfestors" to push the remaining inhabitants out of the Bronx by any means necessary, fire and gas included, in order to tear it down and rebuild it into an expensive new "city of the future". The movie follows biker hero Trash – played by Mark Gregory, a then eighteen-year-old bodybuilder Castellari met at his gym in Rome – as he joins a motley crew of mercenaries, reporters and surviving gang members who plan to kidnap the president of the evil General Construction corporation.

The contribution of the "Italian Roger Cormans" to our futurama of doomsday scenarios is made all the more colorful by their previous experiences in a wide variety of film genres – from peplum to western, giallo, horror and gore. Castellari and Martino were strong in exploring the fascination with cynicist trigger-happy villains in a lawless no man's land, which their post-atomic wastelands shared with the old West. Joe D'Amato added a gory touch to his *Endgame* by lingering on the gruesome details of a society sliding into uncontrolled violence and survival of the cruelest. Lucio Fulci, coming from a string of successful horror movies that elevated him to cult legend, nailed the atmospheres of his *Warriors of the Year 2072* by referencing Corman's *Pit and the Pendulum* in an *Alphaville*-inspired plot twist, depicting Rome as a glacial plexiglass-covered megalopolis dominated by an artificial intelligence bent on controlling mankind through virtual-reality experiences of medieval torture.

There Is No Future, The Future Is Now

If we slide fifty years back in time through the wormhole opened by their beautifully ominous synth-fueled soundtracks, the elaborate medley of imagined universes brought to us by these movies can work its way through the haze of our own visions of future horror, merging them in a kaleidoscope of shared representations of apocalyptic scenarios. They make a great companion for reflective late nights spent contemplating our vain illusions of control, our increasingly grim prospects and the mindless late-capitalist routines we perform, leaving us unable to swim against the insanity of it all.

Part of what makes post-apocalyptic movies feel realistic is that they never show mankind having learned a lesson from their past, ever: more often than not, the fall of our civilization is self-inflicted, and a return to the "state of nature" is inevitable – after all, that's what we were taught to expect if the institutions that currently govern our society should cease to exist. However, one of the great virtues of movies, as Claudio Simonetti put it, is that they allow us to explore universes and atmospheres we wouldn't be able to access otherwise. What if we refused to fulfill the role set in place for us by our 'masters' and chose to write our own destiny, much like Paco Queruak, the unwavering, rebellious cyborg portrayed by Daniel Greene in Sergio Martino's *Hands of Steel*? There may be few chances left for mankind to abandon the good old *"homo homini lupus"* motto before our time is over, but there is still some room for elevating ourselves above it, by using the best tools at our disposal – such as art, science and education – or simply by practicing the most rewarding yet elusive of skills: the ability to truly open our minds to other perspectives.

Italian Post-Atomic Movies

- *1990: The Bronx Warriors (1990: I guerrieri del Bronx)*
  Enzo G. Castellari, 1982

- *Warriors Of The Year 2072 (I guerrieri dell'anno 2072)*
  Lucio Fulci, 1982

- *The New Barbarians (I nuovi barbari)*
  Enzo G. Castellari, 1983

- *Escape From The Bronx (Fuga dal Bronx)*
  Enzo G. Castellari, 1983

- *2019, After The Fall Of New York (2019 – Dopo la caduta di New York)*
  Sergio Martino (Martin Dolman), 1983

- *Yor, The Hunter From The Future (Il mondo di Yor)*
  Antonio Margheriti (Anthony M. Dawson), 1983

- *Endgame (Endgame – Bronx lotta finale)*
  Joe D'Amato, 1983

- *Atlantis Interceptors (I predatori di Atlantide)*
  Ruggero Deodato, 1983

- *2020 Texas Gladiators (Anno 2020 – I gladiatori del futuro)*
  Joe D'Amato, 1984

- *Hands Of Steel (Vendetta dal futuro)*
  Sergio Martino, 1986

TERROR UND TRANSGRESSION IM NIEMANDSLAND

Die Filme von Takahisa Zeze

---

von Christian Lenz

Takahisa Zeze ist einer der profiliertesten und produktivsten japanischen Filmemacher der Gegenwart. Mehr als sechzig Arbeiten konnte der Regisseur seit Ende der 1980er-Jahre realisieren, darunter Blockbuster wie der zweiteilige Mystery-Krimi *Roku yon* (*64*, 2016) oder das slicke Liebesdrama *8-nengoshi no Hanayome: Kiseki no Jitsuwa* (*The 8-Year Engagement*, 2017). Aber auch transgressive Erotikfilm-Miniaturen und auf besondere Weise quer zum konventionalisierten Formen- und Themenrepertoire des Populärkinos stehende Projekte zählen zu Zezes Werk; etwa die über fünfstündige, mäandernde *Documentary Zunō keisatsu* (2009) über Reunion-Bemühungen der titelgebenden Proto-Punk-Band, die auf eine bewegte Geschichte zwischen Fansuiziden und den terroristischen Ausläufern der 70er-Jahre-APO zurückblicken kann.

Außerhalb seines Heimatlandes ist Zezes Œuvre hingegen immer noch kaum bekannt. Zwar waren einige seiner Arbeiten von Cannes bis Berlin auf renommierten europäischen Festivals zu sehen, reguläre Kinostarts erhielten die Filme außerhalb Japans jedoch nicht. Nur wenige sind als untertitelte Heimmedien-Veröffentlichungen greifbar, und selbst klandestine Online-Gegenarchive bleiben insbesondere im Hinblick auf das Frühwerk lückenhaft.

Der Grund für diese Leerstellen dürfte weniger in der Vielseitigkeit der Filmografie liegen, sondern gerade in ihrer Kohärenz. Im Laufe seiner Karriere hat sich der obsessiv arbeitende Zeze einer Vielzahl an Stoffen, Erzählformen und Genres gewidmet, gleichzeitig bleiben seine Filme aber durch motivische, inszenatorische und geografische Charakteristika über unterschiedlichste Produktionskontexte hinweg miteinander vermittelt – und sperren sich mit finster-buddhistischer Weltsicht und starkem Fokus auf randständige Charaktere auch dann gegenüber einfacher Vermarkt- und Kategorisierbarkeit, wenn sie sich deutlich an etablierten Strategien aus dem Zentrum der Kulturindustrie orientieren. Abseits des humanistischen Festival- und kalkuliert weirden Kultfilms, mit denen das zeitgenössische Nippon-Kino im Ausland vor allem assoziiert ist, hat Zeze seine ganz eigene Sprache und Energie entwickelt.

Takahisa Zeze wurde 1960 in der Präfektur Okinawa auf der Insel Kyūshū geboren und studierte Philosophie an der prestigeträchtigen Kyōto Universität, die zahlreiche Nobelpreisträger zu ihren Absolventen zählt. Bereits während des Studiums drehte er diverse 16mm- und 8mm-Kurzfilme und organisierte Kinoabende auf denen unter anderem die eng mit zeitgenössischen Protestbewegungen verkoppelten Werke des radikalen Dokumentaristen Ogawa Shinsuke gezeigt wurden. Nach seinem Abschluss 1986 assistierte Zeze kurzzeitig bei dem von

Ogawas Filmkollektiv Ogawa Pro realisierten partizipatorischen Langzeitprojekt *1000-nen kizami no hidokei* (*Magino Village: A Tale*, 1987) über eine Reisbauernkooperative. Sein vollständiger Einstieg in die Filmbranche erfolgte im selben Jahr jedoch in einem anderen Bereich der japanischen Kinolandschaft: dem sogenannten *Pinku eiga*, international als Pinkfilm bekannt. Bei diesem singulären Phänomen handelt es sich um Erotikfilme, die kostengünstig von kleinen Independent-Studios für die Kinoauswertung produziert werden und – zumindest bis zur zweiten Hälfte der 2000er – überwiegend auf 35mm gedreht sind. *Pinku eigas* sind dabei kein Nischenprodukt: Nachdem das japanische Kino zu Beginn der 1960er-Jahre unter anderem durch die Einführung des Farbfernsehens an Popularität eingebüßt hatte, führte der enorme Publikumszuspruch für diese neue, aufregende Art des Films die Branche aus der Krise. Unter dem Eindruck des immensen Erfolgs der Pinkus produzierten die Major Studios Nikkatsu und Tōei mit ihren Roman Porno- und Pinky Violence-Zyklen bald Kinoreihen, die auf ähnlich spektakuläre Weise körperliche Schauwerte apostrophierten. Mitte der 1970er-Jahre machten Pinkfilme und angrenzende Phänomene rund fünfzig Prozent der japanischen Filmproduktion aus und sind bis heute Teil der Populärkultur. *Pinku eiga* meint dabei auch ein spezifisches Auswertungs- und Distributionssystem, das Filmen weitreichende Verbreitung über die Zusammenarbeit von Studios mit spezialisierten Kinoketten sichert, vor allem aber einen bestimmten Produktionsmodus, der Regisseuren kreative Freiheit eingesteht, solange sie die Minimalanforderung von mehreren Softcore-Sexszenen – rund eine alle zehn Minuten – bei einer durchschnittlichen Spielzeit von etwas mehr als einer Stunde einhalten. Dementsprechend entwickelte sich das Pinku-Segment schnell zu einem Karrieresprungbrett und Experimentierfeld für aufstrebende Filmemacher, die stilistische Innovation und subversive Polit-Subtexte wagten.

Takahisa Zeze assistierte zunächst bei drei auf ein schwules Publikum zugeschnittenen Produktionen von Hisayasu Satō für das Pink-Studio Shishi Pro und schrieb Drehbücher für *S&M Hunter*-Regisseur Shuji Kataoka, bevor 1989 mit *Kagai jugyō: Bōkō* (*Go to Haneda and You Will See Kids Dressed Like Pirates Ready to Attack*) sein erster eigener Langfilm veröffentlicht wurde.

Bereits dieses Debüt machte deutlich, dass der mit politisch engagiertem Protestkino sozialisierte Regisseur angetreten war, den künstlerischen Spielraum des Produktionskontexts auf besondere Weise zu nutzen. In den Erotikfilm-Rahmen trägt Zeze unter anderem die tragische Liebesgeschichte zwischen einem Angehörigen der koreanischen Minderheit und einer taiwanesischen Prostituierten ein und wendet sich auf zuvor beispiellos offensive Manier der Ausgrenzung zu, die verarmte asiatische Migrantenmilieus in Japan erfahren – ein Problemkomplex, der den Filmemacher im Laufe seiner Karriere immer wieder beschäftigen sollte. Markant ist dabei bereits Zezes Vorliebe für allegorisch aufgeladene Landschaften, deren Abgelegenheit und transitorischer Charakter – im konkreten Fall eine weder ganz dem Land noch Wasser zugehörige Pfahlbausiedlung in der Nähe des Flughafens Tokio-Haneda – mit den Identitätskrisen und der sozialen Isolation seiner Filmfiguren korrespondieren. Den Eindruck, den diese Orte hinterlassen, pointiert der englische Titel des mit ausgestellten Godard-Referenzen versehenen, verspielten Nachfolgewerks *Waisetsu bōsō shūdan: Kemono* (*No Man's Land*, 1991).

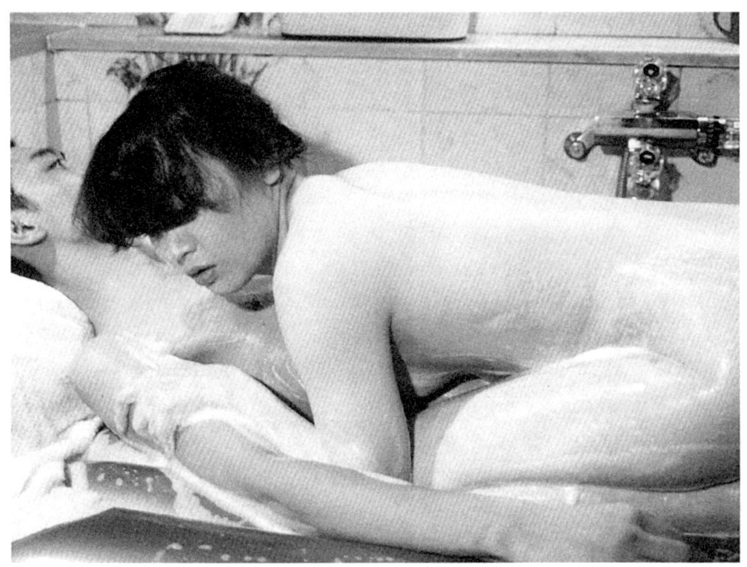

Bis 1996 realisierte Zeze sechzehn Erotikfilmproduktionen, die allesamt für Kokuei entstanden, einem der ältesten Genrestudios, das lange Zeit von der Produzentin Keiko Sato unter dem Männerpseudonym Asakura Daisuke geführt wurde. Als einziges Werk dieses initialen Pinkruns schaffte es mit *Kōkyō Soap Technique 4: Monzetsu higi* (*The Dream of Garuda*, 1994) ein bemerkenswert finster-transgressiver Brocken auf ein (stark gekürztes) untertiteltes DVD-Release. Das mit mythologischer Schwere und Vergewaltigungsthematik Widerhaken in Richtung Leichtverdaulichkeit werfende Werk ist gleichzeitig der vierte Teil eines losen *Soap Technique*-Zyklus und setzt mit spektakulärer Lotion Play-Akrobatik Höhepunkte.

Die restlichen Kokuei-Produktionen bleiben außerhalb Japans weitestgehend unsichtbar – darunter viele Meisterwerke wie der somnambul-elegische *Lesbian eiga-*

Doppelschlag *Kindan no sono: The seifuku lesbian* (*Amazon Garden: Uniform Lesbians*, 1992) und *Honban lesbian: Hazukashi taii* (*September's Fallen Angel*, 1994) oder die Vulkaninsel-Amour Fou *Sukebe tenkomori* (*End of the World*, 1994) um ein farcenhaft asoziales Gangsterpärchen und ihren Hahn, der im Schlussakt abgefackelt wird.

Auf Akteursebene gilt Zezes Interesse von Beginn an den Ausgestoßenen und Delinquenten – Kleinganoven, Bombenbauern und desillusionierten Driftern. Mit ungewöhnlichen Einstellungswinkeln, expressiver Tongestaltung und halluzinogenen Experimental-Sequenzen beweisen seine Pinku-Beiträge unbedingten Stilwillen und changieren in elliptisch-kompakter Form souverän zwischen Narration und Nummer. Die ambitionierte künstlerische Signatur seiner Frühwerke brachte dem Regisseur das Label als einer der vier *pinku shitenno* ein, was sowohl mit *Devils* als auch *Heavenly Kings of Pink* übersetzt wurde. Gemeint sind damit neben Zeze die Kokuei-Regisseure Kazuhiro Sano sowie Hisayasu und Toshiki Satô, die sich auf ähnlich wild-innovative Weise der Erotikfilmproduktion verschrieben; mitunter wurde in Anlehnung an die französische Kinoerneuerungsbewegung auch von einer *Pink Nouvelle Vague* gesprochen. Alle diese Filmemacher starteten ihre Karrieren gegen Ende der 1980er-Jahre zu einem Zeitpunkt, als die Hochphase des *Pinku eigas* im Grunde schon beendet war. Nicht zuletzt die zunehmende Verbreitung von Videoequipment und eine daraus resultierende Proliferation von Hardcore Pornografie hatte das Interesse an entsprechenden Kinofilmen abflauen lassen, gleichzeitig riss der Bankrott des zuletzt fast ausschließlich auf Roman Pornos spezialisierten Großstudios Nikkatsu eine signifikante Lücke in die nationale Filmproduktion, die zumindest kurzzeitig die Möglichkeit für neue, junge Regisseure eröffnete, ihre

Werke auf dem Markt zu platzieren. Der Nonkonformismus der *Four Devils* war dabei eigentlich als letztes kreatives Aufbäumen vor dem sich abzeichnenden Untergang des Pinkfilms geplant, wie sich Zeze später in einem Interview erinnerte: »Wir spürten, dass der Pinkfilm akut vom Aussterben bedroht war, also dachte ich, wenn er sowieso verschwindet, dann wird man uns auch machen lassen, was wir wollen.« Tatsächlich leiteten aber insbesondere Zezes innovative Werke eine regelrechte Renaissance des *Pinku eiga* ein: Sie waren nicht nur kommerziell erfolgreich, sondern lenkten desweiteren ungeahntes Interesse der japanischen wie internationalen Cinephilie auf das Segment. Als erste Filme dieses Zuschnitts liefen sie 1993 in der renommierten Tokioer Kulturinstitution Athénée Français und wurden fortan sowohl in Pink- als auch Arthouse-Spielstätten ausgewertet sowie in japanischen Kinokompendien neben kanonischen Regisseuren wie Akira Kuroswa oder Nagisa Ōshima diskutiert. Erste ausländische Screenings folgten eher spät, ab Mitte der Neunzigerjahre auf dem Rotterdamer Filmfestival und der Viennale.

Der Erfolg von Zezes *Pinku eiga*-Beiträgen ermöglichte es ihm bald, sich in weiteren Bereichen zu verwirklichen. 1997 erschien, nochmals für Kokuei, das tieftraurige Karriere-Highlight *Raigyo*, das mit 75 Minuten Spielzeit, vergleichsweise hohem Budget und niedrigem Sexszenenanteil über das Genre-Korsett hinausweist und dem 2004, mit dem ähnlich bewegenden wie narrativ entschlackten Post-Pinku *Hada no sukima* (*A Gap in the Skin*), ein Quasi-Schwesterfilm zur Seite gestellt wurde. *Raigyo* ist nach einer unessbaren Schlangenkopf-Fischart benannt, die parasitäre Würmer in sich trägt und ursprünglich aus Taiwan nach Japan eingeschleppt wurde. In den Anfangsbildern des Films verbrennt ein Fischer Exemplare der für ihn wertlosen Art, in *Hada no sukima* werden die Tiere in einigen neuralgischen Stellen gleich kamerawirksam mit einem Stein zermatscht – beide Werke setzen mit entsprechenden Bildern die Stimmung für ihre bedingungslos hoffnungslosen Geschichten um zerrüttete Messermörder, die letztlich selbst unter die Räder geraten.

Ebenfalls 1997 wurde die erste eindeutige Nicht-Pinku-Arbeit veröffentlicht. Das, wie viele Zeze-Filme, aus dezidiert weiblicher Perspektive erzählte Geister-Werk *Kokkuri-san* nimmt Motive aus den J-Horror-Hits *Ringu* (1998) und *Juon* (2002) vorweg, überzeugt abseits traditioneller Schockmomente und drastischer Effekte aber vor allem als leises Traumabewältigungs- und lesbisches Liebes-Drama. Darüber hinaus teilt es mit *Raigyo* sympathischerweise den tief sitzenden Pessimismus und setzt mit seiner komplexen Flashback-Struktur den künstlerisch ambitionierten Stil des Regisseurs fort.

Fantastische Werke, die sich auf originelle Weise Genre-Stoffen annähern, bleiben eine Konstante in Takahisa Zezes Œuvre: Der komödiantische Science-Fiction-Beitrag *SF Whipped Cream* (2002) baut die Geschichte auf der Erde gestrandeter Außerirdischer zur antirassistischen Parabel aus: ein Motiv, das in dem Vampir-Drama *Moon Child* (2003) invertiert wird. Diese als Vehikel für die Popstars HYDE und Gackt angelegte Dystopie erzählt von illegalen japanisch-stämmigen Straßenkindern in einer fiktiven trans-asiatischen Zukunftsmetropole und weist mit dem angedeuteten homosexuellen Begehren zwischen den beiden Protagonisten gleichzeitig auf Zezes Anfänge in der Filmbranche zurück. Über die Jahre folgten mit Stars besetzte, hochbudgetierte Großproduktionen, die Zeze in Japan endgültig einem Massenpublikum bekannt machten, darunter der Seuchen-Thriller *Kansen rettô* (*Pandemic*, 2009) und mehrere Liebesfilme. Der größte Hit, das Krankheitsdrama *8-nengoshi no Hanayome: Kiseki no Jitsuwa* (*The 8-Year Engagement*, 2017), setzt mit einigen horrorfilmartigen Visualisierungen von Epilepsiezuständen zugegebenermaßen eher auf spärliche Art und Weise eigene Akzente.

Zezes Filmografie geht jedoch in keiner klaren Phasen-Chronologie auf – immer wieder zieht es den Regisseur zu seinen *Pinku eiga*-Anfängen zurück, zuletzt vollumfänglich in der extravaganten Mystery-Moritat *Maria no chibusa* (*Maria's Breasts*, 2014) um eine Prostituierte mit hellseherischen Kräften oder bereits 2001 mit dem provokanten *Tōkyō X Erotica*, der medienreflexive Episoden und zeitgeschichtliche Verweise auf die Terroranschläge der Aum-Sekte in sein spekulatives Erotikfilm-Setting integriert (und trotz seiner besonders nonkonformistischen Gestaltungssignatur aus Cinéma Vérité-artigen Einschüben und roh-instabilen DV-Bildern das einzige Zeze-Werk ist, das jemals im deutschen Fernsehen lief – 2011, nachts auf arte).

Die Konstanz, mit der Zeze in unterschiedlichen etablierten Produktionskontexten reüssiert, erlaubt es ihm zudem nun häufiger, unabhängig realisierte, persönliche Projekte zu verwirklichen, die auf besondere Weise erzählökonomische Erfordernisse des Mainstream-Kinos und generische Erwartungshaltungen unterlaufen. Hervorzuheben sind das bisher kaum aufgeführte, widerspenstige Episodenwerk *Nariyuki na tamashii* (*Random Lives*, 2016), das den Regisseur mit einer hervorragend aus dem Ruder laufenden gewalttätigen Montage-Sequenz in Karriere-Bestform zeigt sowie das 278 Minuten lange, bewegende Ensemble-Rache-Drama *Hevunzu sutôr* (*Heaven's Story*, 2010) und der im Nachgang des verheerenden Kantō-

Erdbebens von 1923 spielende dreistündige *Kiku to Guillotine. Onnazumō to Anarchist* (*The Chrysanthemum and the Guillotine*, 2018) – ein hochenergetischer Historienfilm, in dem die Geschichten einer Gruppe Sumo-Ringerinnen und der anarchistischen Terrorgang Guillotine Society in einem bei Zeze dauerpräsenten Topos kulminieren: der verzweifelten Rebellion gegen die Determinierung des Lebens durch Schicksal und Tradition.

Einen weiteren, bisher kaum erschlossenen Nebenstrang in Zezes Werk bilden seine dokumentarischen Arbeiten, die vor allem für das japanische Fernsehen produziert wurden und dort unter Verschluss liegen. In den letzten Jahren weitete sich die Kooperation mit TV-Anstalten zudem auf Serien-Projekte aus, darunter eine fünfteilige Remake-Variation des US-amerikanischen Erfolg-Formats *Cold Case*.

Auf den ersten Blick liegt die Vermutung nah, dass mit Zezes zunehmenden Vorstößen in etablierte Entertainmentbereiche die Eigentümlichkeit seines Werks verloren gegangen ist oder es zumindest eine klare Ausdifferenzierung erfährt – in kommerzielle Ausstoßware einerseits und künstlerisch versierte Herzensprojekte andererseits. (Diese Demarkationslinie wird nicht nur in den wenigen englischsprachigen Texten über Zeze stets angedeutet.) Dafür spricht auch, dass marktdominante japanische Filmstudios seit Jahren ein Produktionskomitee-System implementiert haben. Die finale Gestaltung von Blockbustern findet dort in Abstimmung verschiedener Vertragspartner und vor allem mit Blick auf eine möglichst breite Auswertung im Rahmen transmedialer Franchise-Projekte statt. Einer genaueren Auseinandersetzung mit Zezes Gesamtwerk hält die Idee einer eindeutigen Aufteilung der Filmografie jedoch nicht stand.

Zezes fantastische Genre-Beiträge bevölkern größtenteils zwischen den Welten stehende Figuren – von der Protagonistin in *Kokkuri-san*, die unbemerkt von ihren Schulfreundinnen eine Parallel-Existenz als Radiostar führt und per Hexenbrett den Kontakt zur Geistersphäre sucht, bis zu Mutanten-Teenagern mit übersinnlich-animalischen Fähigkeiten im Clinch mit den japanischen Autoritäten in der erstaunlich finsteren Jugendbuch-Adaption (und *X Men*-Variation) *Sutoreiyâzu kuronikuru* (*Strayer's Chronicle*, 2015), die mit dem in Vernichtungsplänen mündenden Menschenverdruss ihres Antagonisten nie völlig ausräumt. Grenzgänger bilden ebenfalls das Gravitationszentrum des Festivalhits *Hevunzu sutôr*, der unter anderem das Schicksal eines Polizisten verfolgt, der nebenbei als Auftragskiller arbeitet. Die bis dato letztveröffentlichte Arbeit, das Mütterdrama *Ashita no Shokutaku* (*Tomorrow's Dining Table*, 2021), eine aufwendig für den Medienkonzern Kadokawa produzierte und klassisch inszenierte Literaturverfilmung mit TV-Stars in den Hauptrollen, zeigt unter anderem mit empathischen Blick auf eine Kindsmörderin und dem Übergriff eines 10-Jährigen auf seine demenzkranke Oma, dass auch das Zentrum des japanischen Mainstreams ein Niemandsland sein kann und Terror und Transgression in konventionellen filmischen Formen heimisch werden können.

Oft sind es transitorische, abgelegene Orte, an denen sich die ungewöhnlichen Geschichten von Zezes randständigen Charaktere vollziehen: Die Pfahlbau-Siedlungen nahe des Flughafens Tokio-Haneda, Wohnort der *urban poor*, bilden neben dem erwähnten Pinkfilm-Debüt auch das Setting der TV-Dokumentation *The Memory of Water: Private Landscapes of Haneda* (1996) sowie für die quirlige Verwechslungskomödie *Furaingu rabittsu* (*Flying Rabbits*, 2008) um ein Team von

Basketballspielerinnen. Die Wünsche und Hoffnungen von Zezes Protagonisten können innerhalb der Grenzen dieser sozialen wie geografischen Peripherie häufig nicht ausgestaltet werden. Nicht selten enden selbst seine realistisch orientierten Filme daher in Traum- und Mystiksequenzen, die durch mal mehr, mal weniger eindeutige Ausgestaltung des Transzendentalen eine unüberbrückbare Lücke markieren zwischen den Aspirationen dieser grenzgängerischen Figuren und den begrenzenden Milieus, in die sie eingepflanzt sind. Fluchtpunkt ist dabei meist ein buddhistisch-nihilistisches Gefühl für Vergänglichkeit: Katastrophen passieren, Menschen sterben und werden (wieder-)geboren; die Welt ist überwiegend scheiße und frustrierend, bleibt jedoch im Fluss.

Die Beharrlichkeit, mit der Zeze entlang diverser Stoffe und verschiedener Zeiträume – von der späten Taishō-Ära in *Kiku to Guillotine. Onnazumō to Anarchist* bis zu der nahen Zukunft in etwa *Tōkyō X Erotica* – japanische Geschichte konsequent von den gesellschaftlichen Rändern aus erzählt, tritt dabei im vollen Umfang hervor, wenn man die Karriere des Regisseurs über unterschiedliche Produktionskontexte hinweg verfolgt. Es zeichnet sich der Horizont einer vielstimmigen, nonlinearen Gegengeschichte ab, die abseits Exklusionstendenzen traditioneller Sichtbarkeitsverhältnisse jene Perspektiven in den Mittelpunkt rückt, die ansonsten jenseits der öffentlichen Wahrnehmung situiert sind. Dazu passt, dass Zeze Filmstoffe häufig Kurzmeldungen über Verbrechen und Schicksalsschläge in Boulevard-Zeitungen entnommen sind, seine Alternativ-Geschichte sich also aus dem vermeintlich Obsoleten und Kurzlebigen assembliert.

Mit weitreichenden historischen Spuren sind dabei auch jene Werke imprägniert, die besonders unmittelbar auf ihre Entstehungszeit reagieren: Ruinen aus der prosperierenden Shōwa-Ära durchziehen die Stadtrand-Settings insbesondere der frühen *Pinku eiga*-Arbeiten, die zu einem Zeitpunkt veröffentlicht wurden, als die Orientierungslosigkeit und materielle Not ihrer Figuren durch die Implosion der japanischen Bubble-Ökonomie längst breite Bevölkerungsschichten erreicht hatte. Die Showdowns sowohl des unabhängig mit geringsten Mitteln realisierten *Hevunzu sutôr* als auch der kapitalintensiven Warner Bros.-Produktion *Sutoreiyâzu kuronikuru* finden dann markanterweise in den zum Skelett ausgehöhlten Überresten eines Danchi-Hochhausgebäudes statt, wie sie in den 1960er-Jahren einst emblematisch für den japanischen Wirtschaftsaufschwung standen. Zezes unkonventioneller Modus sich im filmischen Medium auf historische Schichten zu beziehen korrespondiert dabei mit dem ungewöhnlichen Verlauf seiner Regiekarriere: Seine Grenzgänge zwischen unterschiedlichsten Genres und Stoffen montieren sich in der Gesamtschau zu einer alternativen Filmgeschichte mit der vielfältige Erscheinungsformen des japanischen Kinos der letzten dreißig Jahre genauso wie Abweichungschancen in vermeintlich konsolidierten Produktionszusammenhängen hervortreten.

English version available at laerm-publications.com

Recommended Takahisa Zeze Movies

- *Hada no sukima (A Gap in the Skin),* 2004
- *Kuroi shitagi no onna: Raigyo,* 1997
- *Kindan no sono: The Seifuku Lesbian (Amazon Garden: Uniform Lesbians a.k.a. The Phenomenon of me is the Blue Illumination of one of the Hypothetical Organic AC Lamps),* 1992
- *Kiku to Guillotine. Onnazumō to Anarchist (The Chrysanthemum and the Guillotine)*, 2018
- *Kōkyō Soap Technique 4: Monzetsu higi (The Dream of Garuda aka High Class Bathhouse Sex Technique: Blissful Secret Acts),* 1994
- *Hevunzu sutôrî (Heaven's Story),* 2010
- *Sukebe tenkomori (End of the World),* 1995
- *Honban lesbian: Hazukashi taii (Fallen Angels in September),* 1994
- *Nariyuki na tamashii (Random Lives),* 2016
- *Anaakii in Japansuke: Mirarete iku onna (Anarchy in Japansuke: God, You Are Just Useless)*, 2019

The white woman, if she be married to the red man,
presently they embrace, and embracing are coupled.
By themselves they are dissolved and by themselves
they are brought together, that they which were two,
may be made as it were one body.

Son, by the faith of the glorious God,
complexion is of Complexion, between two lights,
male and female, and then they embrace themselves
and couple together,
and a perfect light is begotten between them,
which there is no light like through the whole world.

The Rosary of the Philosophers, 1550

THE MYSTERY OF THE GOLDEN EGG

An alchemical reading of George Sluizer's *Spoorloos*

by Rumen Lasev

The following text will be discussing the film Spoorloos (The Vanishing) *in great detail. It is a film that has an undeniably impactful ending, which will be extensively analyzed and referenced numerous times. Let this serve as a warning for anyone who has never seen the film and wishes to go into it blind.*

In 1988 George Sluizer shook the world of European cinema with his "unforgettably chilling psychodrama" *Spoorloos*[1] (*The Vanishing*). In Europe, it received immediate critical acclaim and won numerous awards. Sluizer's masterful direction was praised by both critics and other film makers. Stanley Kubrick himself declared the film to be much more frightening than *The Shining* and even got in touch with Sluizer to discuss editing. Naturally, when dealing with a mystery/thriller such as *Spoorloos*, comparisons to Alfred Hitchcock are inevitable; it was recognized by some to be the "ultimate tribute" to the master of suspense. Specific attention was drawn to the final denouement, which manages to dwarf even some of Hitchcock's most memorable endings.

The film tells the story of a young and adoring Dutch

couple, Saskia Wagter (Johanna ter Steege[2]) and Rex Hofman[3] (Gene Bervoets) who are on their way to a biking vacation in Bois Veaux[4], France (an incredibly fitting name for the somewhat archaic allusions the film makes). As they enter a tunnel, Saskia opens up about a recurring ominous dream she has been having in which she's drifting through space in a golden egg. However, in her most recent dream, a second egg containing another person appeared. The eventual and inevitable collision of the two is something that causes Saskia to be somewhat anxious and morbid, as she feels that it signifies the end of something and that it might soon become a reality. In the tunnel, their car runs out of gas, resulting in a heated and tense argument between them, ending with Rex leaving her alone in the car. It is here, in the engulfing darkness, that her sense of the end being nigh peaks. The viewer also feels that this might be the moment in which "the vanishing" itself happens, which contributes to the overall tone of helplessness and despair. However, as it turns out, both the viewer and Saskia are wrong and the couple makes it to a bright and populated rest area, where Saskia mysteriously disappears while buying refreshments. In a brilliantly edited sequence, accompanied by ghastly evocative music, the jolly and summery atmosphere at the gas station suddenly becomes unsettling and chilling. In broad daylight, her inexplicable vanishing leaves both Rex and the viewer completely in the dark. Fast forward three years and Rex has started a new relationship, but he is still obsessively longing to find out what happened to Saskia and is having the same dream about the golden egg. His longing for answers leads him to a downward spiral of obsession, which culminates when the kidnapper, Raymond Lemorne (Bernard-Pierre Donnadieu), contacts him, and the two eventually meet. However, despite Rex and Saskia clearly being the ones suffering throughout the story, the film does not focus the bulk of its attention on them. In fact, she is in the film for a total of 11 minutes. Instead, what Sluizer does is providing the viewer with a window into the workings of an incredibly methodical sociopath, whose identity is revealed early in the film. Raymond is an ordinary high school chemistry teacher, and a loving husband and father – someone rather unremarkable and almost invisible at times. Upon meeting Rex, he offers him the opportunity to find out exactly what happened to Saskia, under the condition that he has to undergo the exact same experience. Reluctant at first, Rex hesitates, but the image of an arduous life filled with dreadful uncertainty pushes him over the edge, and he accepts Raymond's offer. In what is perhaps one of the most memorable reveals and endings in cinema, Rex is shown buried alive, just like Saskia was, in the property of Raymond's family villa. The film concludes with a closing shot of a newspaper headline about the vanishing of Saskia and Rex. The egg-shaped image of each contrasted against the unbearable darkness.

Spoorloos is an intensely visual experience, so I apologize for possibly not being able to do it justice in writing. Everything about the film – from the camera work, score, use of colours and lighting, to the acting and editing – contributes to a memorable and outstanding experience that lingers after the credits roll out. It certainly stands out from others in the mystery/thriller genre and is undoubtedly Sluizer's Magnum Opus. My usage of 'Magnum Opus' here instead of, say, 'masterpiece' is quite deliberate. As it is probably evident from my love for the film, I have indeed seen it multiple times and read up on it extensively. However, even after many viewings, it felt like *Spoorloos* was still hiding something from me.

Something much greater, which maybe I was not yet ready for. Despite supposedly providing all the necessary answers to questions about its characters and plot, it felt like *Spoorloos*, unlike other films within the genre, was asking me questions I did not have the answers for. After each viewing, I felt like the film invited me to revisit it once I had more to bring to the table. It was not until years later when I started learning more about alchemy, its history and philosophy, that my mind suddenly felt drawn to tackle the *Mystery of the Golden Egg* once more. It almost felt like some external force was directing my mind to passively think about the film. So I did, and by the end of the film, I felt as if all the praise that the film has received was still insufficient to describe just how masterfully crafted it is. The idea of looking at *Spoorloos* not only as a Magnum Opus in the modern meaning (an artist's great work) but in the alchemical sense was what drew me to have a different set of questions prepared for the next time I watched the film. I would not claim to have all the answers to the riddle of the golden egg now, but what I hope to do is offer a different reading from a slightly new perspective, which may seem unorthodox at first glance. When I revisit *Spoorloos* now, I mostly view it as a story about alchemy wrapped in a thriller/mystery package, rather than the other way around. The elements of both are there, and certainly, the film could exist on its own as a genre film if all the symbology and allusions to alchemy were removed. However, without them, *Spoorloos* would lose most of what drives the film's eerie atmosphere, and the effect that the characters – especially Raymond Lemorne – have on the viewer.

The alchemical Magnum Opus is a term very closely associated with the creation of the philosopher's stone. The idea was to bring something to perfection, by growing or developing it from a primitive or base form. The classic and most famous example would be the transmutation of base metals, like mercury, to gold. Essentially, alchemy's goal was the creation of higher things via the transformation of lower, inferior things. It was believed that in order to be perfected each substance or element had to be reduced to its most primal state (or materia prima). This took place in the centre of the alchemist's oven or vessel, often symbolically referred to as the philosopher's egg, or the philosophic egg, in which they

aimed to replicate what happens at the bowels of the earth, but at a greater speed, essentially mimicking God's work. Only after placing it in such an embryonic form – *regressus ad uterum* (returning to the womb) – to rid it of its impurities, could the substance then be transmuted and transformed into the sought after perfect paradisaical gold. Because the laboratory arose as the place to imitate nature, most of the experiments were carried out in the centre of a laboratory vessel – analogous to the processes occurring in the centre of the earth, i.e., *in medio centri*. Symbolically speaking though, vials can be seen as the earth's core and vice-versa. The importance of the vessel cannot be overstated. It was no coincidence that such great emphasis was placed on its shape. One usually thinks of a test tube or a flask, but due to the symbolic nature of alchemy itself, the vessel assumed a mystical role, thus becoming a significant symbol, central to many of the alchemical processes. It must be round, preferably egg-shaped, in order to properly replicate the idea of the spherical cosmos associated with creation – almost reminiscent of a uterus from which the miraculous philosopher's stone is born. In the case of *Spoorloos*, the two principal ingredients – mercury and sulfur (Saskia and Rex) are literally placed within the (al)chemist's vial (the bowels of the earth), where they undergo a physical transformation, turning them into gold.

Gold was considered God's element. One that could not corrode or become corrupted; in a way, the material, physical representation of God's qualities. Metals were seen as the most perfect manifestation of basic matter. Aristotle mentions it in book III of *Meteorology*, remarking that the formation of metals comes from two substances. The first one being a watery vapour – most probably mercury – and the second one an earthly smoke – probably sulfur. The idea was that all things are eventually grown to perfection; they mature, ripen into gold; akin to what happens in nature. Alchemists looked for something to catalyze this natural process. Meaning, if mercury and sulfur were in a perfectly pure state, free of their impurities, then the end product would be the most perfect metal – gold. Moreover, the philosopher's stone was also believed to have an effect on the body and the soul. At its core, the idea behind it connects the material and the organic with the spiritual and immaterial. One could argue that the goal was to elevate one to perfection, bringing one closer to God. This was thought to be the ultimate secret, so they resorted to alienating their texts and works as much as possible. The idea was that such secret and powerful knowledge should be kept out of the hands of the vulgar (the unadept, the common people). The language used was generally very cryptic, secretive, symbolic, and coded. A famous example of such language can be seen in the German physician and alchemist Heinrich Khunrath's texts on alchemy:

> *Darkness will appear on the face of the Abyss; Night, Saturn and the Antimony of the Sages will appear; blackness, and the raven's head of the alchemists, and all the colours of the world, will appear at the hour of conjunction; the rainbow also, and the peacock's tail. Finally, after the matter has passed from ashen-coloured to white and yellow, you will see the Philosopher's Stone.*

This quest for the Magnum Opus is what I had in mind when I revisited *Spoorloos* last. An obsessive quest for the great work, whose aim is to elevate something to divine perfection by transmuting it to gold in the alchemical vessel, coded behind the language of the mystery/thriller genre as well as cinema. To my greatest satisfaction, this is what I found.

From its very beginning, *Spoorloos* makes us aware that it's a film that will be reliant on symbology and metaphors, which is of course not uncommon for films in general. If we are to go down the path of alchemy and the nature of the old alchemical texts, we have to accept that the film will explicitly use subverted language and hidden symbology to convey its real meaning. Thus, what is ordinary and seemingly a throwaway reference, or just mere oddity, shouldn't be lightly dismissed. On the contrary, such elements and choices should be viewed

2

as deliberately interwoven into the film's fabric. Some of these symbols might appear almost archaic or arcane to contemporary viewers, but the spiritual symbolism is still there. In that sense, by being imbued with scattered symbols through its entirety, *Spoorloos* mimics how older alchemical texts used to conceal their true meaning behind incredibly allegorical illustrations or incomprehensibly cryptic language. In fact, to further draw this analogy between *Spoorloos* and old alchemical texts, Raymond Lemorne recounts a childhood memory in which he is seen reading the *Mutus Liber* – a seventeenth-century book of illustrated plates dedicated to alchemy. It shows the young boy flipping through its pages, enchanted by what is shown to him. The fifteen plates in the *Mutus Liber* show how one can achieve the Magnum Opus and obtain the philosopher's stone. Explicit focus is put on the second plate where one can clearly see a man and a woman inside a round vessel (philosophical egg). Having gone through the book, young Raymond stands on his balcony in a christ-like position – a stance observed numerous times throughout the film – and decides to jump off. If we follow the notion that Raymond has access to old and arcane knowledge and essentially has the "formula" for the Magnum Opus, and we accept the idea that he is indeed an alchemist working towards its attainment, then any way of viewing the film other than as an old and arcane alchemical text modified to the medium of cinema, will be inadequate and will do a great injustice to the direct references to alchemy that are undeniably present in the film.

Having said all that, the decision to make Raymond the primary focalizer[5] of *Spoorloos*' story is much more than a mere stylistic choice in order to differentiate the film from the conventions of mysteries and thrillers. His main occupation as high-school chemistry teacher is a detail not at all incidental. Despite the fact that in the modern world alchemists are thought to have been charlatans and crazy "crackpot scientists" obsessed with making gold, two of the most prolific modern scientists, Isaac Newton and Robert Boyle, were both heavily influenced by alchemy; the latter of who is considered by many to be the father of chemistry as we know it today. Thus, the connection between alchemy and chemistry cannot be ignored, regardless of whether one believes chemistry to be a direct continuation of alchemy or not.

Perhaps the most prominent and recurring symbol in *Spoorloos* is the golden egg or just oval-shaped things in general – mostly emphasized by Saskia's dream of the golden egg, the bicycles on top of the car, the yellow frisbee, the tunnel. It happens to be one of the most commonly used symbols in alchemy as well. Usually, such circulatory iconography is seen as a way to depict alchemical vessels respectively the philosophic egg. The ambivalence of Saskia's dream only increases the menacing sense it carries, and one cannot help but feel as if it's a *somnia a Deo missa* (a dream sent by God). As they enter the tunnel, it feels like we're stepping into Saskia's inner world: one that is full of fear, her faith is predetermined and in the hands of God. In fact, *Spoorloos* foreshadows Saskia's fate by showing us many images alluding to her death – more specifically death as a way of transcendence. She's seen at the end of the tunnel inside a metaphorical, glowing egg, and on numerous occasions, she's shown looking towards the sky or being in a purposely overexposed frame indicating her movement towards the light. Despite her funny, outgoing, and incredibly charming character, her subconscious appears dark and full of anxiety. According to C.G. Jung, the self itself is a "union of opposites" par excellence; absolutely paradoxical and capable of representing thesis and antithesis simultaneously. We see this being heavily alluded to with the tunnel scene, where the film sets up the primary dichotomies and opposites and unites them. Reality versus dream, light versus darkness, life versus death, male versus female. It is no coincidence that Rex and Saskia have a heated argument while they're in the tunnel. The contrast between both of their characters is astoundingly evident here: Saskia's passivity and timidness against Rex's fiery, volatile outbursts. In alchemy, the "unity of opposites" or *coincidentia oppositorum*, is a mode of thought part of a dialect philosophy, which is most deeply concerned with the creation or existence of something out of at least two opposite, yet dependent conditions. Examples of that would be masculine and feminine; anima and animus; body and soul; mercury and sulfur; etc. The perfect unity of these contrasting pairs was often believed to result in the alchemical Magnum Opus – the philosopher's stone. The allegory of the marriage between the red king and the white queen is an example of one of the most notable unities of opposites in alchemy. The king being sulfur with its combustibility, represented by his masculine, active and blazing persona, while the queen is associated with

mercury and its fusibility, represented by her fluidity, and passivity. Taking the nature of their characters, and the symbology which alchemy uses for mercury and sulfur, it doesn't seem like too much of a stretch to equate each of these two elements to Saskia and Rex respectively – the two principal ingredients of Raymond Lemorne's Magnum Opus.

With all that in mind, it would seem almost ignorant to neglect the signs pointing to Raymond being the grand alchemist in *Spoorloos*. He's the alchemical godhead, the chemist with the book, the possessor of the hidden knowledge that is concealed even from the viewer. As such, he shows that he's capable of turning an egg into gold regardless of whether killing is part of the alchemical transmutation. Lemorne's obsession with his great work is illustrated in the conversation he has with his wife who thinks he's having an affair because of the added mileage to the car, and the time he spends at an isolated house that he's purchased at Saint-Côme[6]. His response to this perfectly encapsulates the pursuit and obsession over something great and echoes the alchemists' philosophy.

> *The house at St. Côme is like a passion. Because it's perfect, it has become a passion. You start with an idea in your head. And you take a step, then a second. Soon, you realize you're up to your neck in something intense… but that doesn't matter. You keep at it for the sheer pleasure of it. For the pure satisfaction it might bring you.*

Disguised as a renovation project, the house is the place where he physically prepares himself for his Magnum Opus. It's an old house that seems like a throwback to earlier times, somewhat reminiscent of a laboratory with all its different flasks and antique containers. We see Lemorne practice various scripts in order to lure a woman into his car, he's adamant about the precision of his movements, and even drugs himself with chloroform to time how long he'll be out. Here we see his incredibly methodical and perfectionist nature; he even makes attempts at developing a basic level of English to aid him in his quest. One of the most unnerving and memorable scenes is when Lemorne picks up his daughter from school and opens the car door for her, walks behind the car, opens the front door with his right hand, as if he's holding a chloroform soaked rag in the other, reaches out behind her to lock the passenger's door, and then "playfully" locks her neck with his right arm, following the exact pattern he's practised for kidnapping. What this creepy sequence demonstrates is that for Raymond there really is no mask of pretence as with most sociopaths. He's not shown as being overly tender and sweet with his family, and ruthlessly violent with his victims. His distant, cold, yet balanced demeanour is persistent, but at the same time, he is also caring. His character is another great example of the "unity of opposites" concept, examples of which we see throughout the whole film. Lemorne is both cruel and loving. Unlike other antagonists in the genre, Raymond's great work is mixed with his normal family life. This indicates that he's a man whose life is in perfect unison and total balance. However, most of the preparations turn out to be futile, as the numerous times he initially attempts to kidnap a woman he actually fails at it. Lemorne even fails at this on the day that they're all at the rest area. In fact, the first time we see him and Saskia engage in a conversation, he seems to have given up on the idea of doing it – he has taken off the false cask from his hand and is simply enjoying a cup of coffee. It almost feels like the whole thing was birthed into fruition by pure chance or faith. However, upon closer scrutiny, we see that there's an astounding amount of events that had to occur in a specific sequence in order for the perfect conditions for Lemorne's Magnum Opus to be achieved. In the initial 15 minutes of *Spoorloos*, we see the two lovers make several decisions, which (maybe not so) indirectly result in the consequential disappearance of Saskia. She actually suggests getting off the highway to see some of the "local colour"; they pass a gas station before entering the tunnel, and Rex dismisses Saskia's concerns about the volume of gas they have; Saskia decides to bury a couple of coins (their change) next to a tree in a superstitious sign of their love. Doing the opposite of any of those would potentially set up a butterfly effect causing Saskia and Lemorne to either never be at the same place, or never have to interact. Despite the perceived randomness of the situation, Saskia's kidnapping almost feels orchestrated by an omnipotent entity, because of how perfectly "the stars had to align" for it occurs. This, combined with the numerous times Raymond is depicted in a crucifix position, alludes to higher powers being at play. At the gas station, Saskia decides to go back and buy them refreshments. Unfortunately, she's out of change, so buying a coffee is suddenly not an option; she asks for some from the other person at the coffee machine, who just happens to be Lemorne. They have a brief exchange, but Saskia eventually goes to the cashier and gets some coins. However, once she‘s got the drinks from the vending machine, she starts a new conversation with him. That's something that might appear unusual but it does seem fitting for Saskia's outgoing personality, and her constant desire to practice her French. She notices Raymond's key chain which bears the letter "R" and asks him whether she could buy it off of him for her boyfriend Rex. Lemorne takes advantage of the situation and says that he's a salesman and has plenty of them in his car. She follows him there and decides to enter the car after seeing a photograph of his family on the car's dashboard. Next thing she knows she's chloroformed and buried alive. What this whole sequence of events demonstrates though, is the reliance on a slightly different vision of the "unity of

opposites" concept in order to not only help advance the film's plot, but Lemorne's Magnum Opus as well. All the elements are there beforehand and explicit attention is paid to them in various scenes before the one at the rest area. For instance, the coins that Saskia and Rex bury right before her demise. It's a scene meant to symbolically represent their endearing love for each other, and it's contrasted with the following scene, leading to her death. Thus, the coins, established as the symbol of love, become a device employed to lead to her death. In turn, the scene in which Raymond is given gifts by his family – tiles for the house at Saint-Côme, a sweater, a key chain with his letter "R", and an album of his life – is contrasted with the sequence where he's at the rest area, looking for a victim. Once again, scenes of endearment and love are contrasted with such which lead to pain and suffering. What really puts the final nail in the coffin both figuratively and literally for Saskia though, is the family photograph that Lemorne takes when he is enjoying a day out with his family. On that day he actually saves a little girl from drowning, further juxtaposing the final and biggest unity of opposites of all – that of life and death. All those gifts and the photograph play a part in completing his Magnum Opus. He wears the sweater on that day, the key chain that Saskia spots, the album is where he gets the inspiration from, the boxes of tiles through which he is pretending to go, looking for a fictitious key chain that is to be sold to Saskia, and finally the family photograph that prompts her to enter the car, thinking that he can be trusted. Symbols of love, affection and the celebration of life become the very tools leading to death. However, even though Lemorne can be an especially cruel alchemical God figure, we must remember that he's also capable of showing love. As such, in killing them he transports them from the material realm to the transcendental plane, where they exist in an untouchable, incorruptible and divinely pure marriage between king and queen.

Despite the critical and popular acclaim of *Spoorloos*, the 1993 Hollywood remake, directed by George Sluizer as well, failed to impress the audiences there. Chiefly because the film was stripped off from all the alchemical, religious, and psychological subtexts, and was instead altered in a more traditional Hollywood fashion. Naturally, the ending was also different. Here, the killer (Jeff Bridges) is vanquished, and the protagonist (Kiefer Sutherland) and his new girlfriend (Sandra Bullock) live happily ever after. Without all the eerie atmosphere and the esoteric and spiritual themes, the film becomes unremarkable and dull. What this shows us is that without those alchemical elements, the true and "real" ending of *Spoorloos* cannot exist. In the end, reading *Spoorloos* via an alchemical key allows us to unlock this almost alternate finale to the film, one that once more echoes the philosophy of unifying opposing qualities. As such, *Spoorloos* allows two endings to coexist simultaneously – a deeply tragic and horrifying one, and one of tranquillity, serenity and transcendental love. Thus, showing us not only the grand alchemist's great work, but the real Magnum Opus as well – one capable of making us feel the unbearable burden of loneliness, knowing that there's no light at the end of the tunnel, and one whose bright shining paradisaical gold comforts us warmly.

Notes

1 Originally based on a novel by Tim Krabbé called *Het Gouden Ei (The Golden Egg)*

2 Her first acting role in a film

3 A fitting and typical alchemical name. A "unity of opposites" – "Rex" meaning "king" and "Hofman" meaning "steward, or one who manages the property of another"

4 "Old woods" in French, which echoes the archaic and arcane undertones of the film

5 A literary term referring to the character through the lens of which the events and the narrative is viewed and presented

6 Saint Cosmas and his brother Saint Damian were Arab physicians and Christian martyrs

Ich wollte an die Kunst glauben als außerstaatliche Lebensqualität.

Gabriele Stötzer

...mehr aber war es wohl der Versuch, [sich] dem Vergessen zu wehren, die Daseinsflüchtigkeit aufzuhalten, Freude und Leid Sinn zu geben

Günter DeBruyn

HINTER MAUERN MEERE

Schreiben und Erinnerung jenseits von DDR-Kulturpolitik
Über Inge Müller und Wolfgang Hilbig

---

von Benedikt Eiden

I.

Der Blick führt über Marmorflächen, vorbei an betäubendem Lila geradewegs in blendende Helle. Irgendwo aus kaputten Baumkronen drängt das irre Gebrüll eines Krähenschwarms, ein paar Fliedergewächse wanken träge im Mittagslicht. Es ist ein angenehm heißer Junitag hier auf dem städtischen Friedhof Berlin-Pankow. Meine Begleitung und ich sind auf den Schotterpfaden des streng duftenden, irgendwie mediterran anmutenden Geländes unterwegs und bereits wieder auf dem Nachhauseweg, als wir plötzlich, nach mehr oder weniger bestrebter Suche, in einem efeuüberwucherten Kiefernhain, die Gedenkstele entdecken. Sie wirkt nüchtern und schmucklos, ist mit seegrüner Patina überzogen. Darauf steht in Typografie einer Schreibmaschine eingraviert: *Inge Müller 1925 – 1966*. Das letzte physische Andenken an eine der »bedeutendsten deutschen Nachkriegslyrikerinnen« tief versteckt im Friedhof, ja verschwindend im trüben Licht zwischen krautigem Wildwuchs und blassgelben Kieferstämmen? Irgendwie, so denken wir, fügt es sich wohl nicht schlecht in diese für lange Zeit übergangene Lebensgeschichte. Dass ihr eigentliches Grab bereits in den frühen Neunzigerjahren abgeräumt und eingeebnet wurde, erfahren wir erst später; niemand wollte anscheinend für die Kosten einer Verlängerung aufkommen.

Ich hatte über Inge Müller zum ersten Mal in Marko Martins unaufgeregter Spurensuche vergessener Ost-Kultur *Die verdrängte Zeit* gelesen, besorgte mir daraufhin die von der Schriftstellerin und ehemaligen DDR-Leichtathletin Ines Geipel verfassten Biografie *Dann fiel auf einmal der Himmel um* und war – naturgemäß – fasziniert von einer zutiefst brüchigen, idealistisch getriebenen Persönlichkeit. Müller trat Mitte der 1950er-Jahre erstmals als Kinderbuch- und Hörspielautorin im Kulturbetrieb der frühen DDR in Erscheinung, verschwand danach jedoch sukzessive aus der öffentlichen Wahrnehmung und blieb, wenn überhaupt, einigen wenigen noch als Ehefrau des heute allseits bekannten Dramatikers Heiner Müller in Erinnerung. Indessen schrieb sie auch eigene Texte, Lyrik und Prosa, von denen zu Lebzeiten – bis auf vereinzelte Abdrucke in zwei Gedichtsammlungen – allerdings kaum etwas publiziert werden konnte. Ob dies aufgrund staatlicher Repressalien geschah oder ob eine umfangreiche Veröffentlichung gar in ihrem Interesse war, scheint bis heute nicht ganz ersichtlich – als Dichterin, die sie letztendlich gewesen ist, blieb sie noch lange über ihren Tod hinaus eine Unbekannte, eine Randnotiz im kanonischen Werk ihres Mannes.

Es sollte ganze zwanzig Jahre dauern, bis 1985 erstmals eine größere Auswahl ihrer Texte bundesweit verlegt werden konnte. Zu diesem Zeitpunkt war Inge Müller in der DDR, zumindest in der Öffentlichkeit, nahezu in Vergessenheit geraten, weshalb die von Dichter Richard Pietraß kompilierte Zusammenstellung im Osten zunächst auch kaum Beachtung fand. In der Bundesrepublik leitete das schmale Bändchen jedoch eine kleine Wiederentdeckung ein: Nach und nach wurde das westliche Feuilleton nun auf die ›schreibende Ehefrau Heiner Müllers‹ aufmerksam: Jenem im Leipziger Aufbau-Verlag erschienenen (wunderbar bibliophilen) Lyrikband *Wenn ich schon sterben muss* folgten über die Jahre hinweg weitere Veröffentlichungen, darunter mehrere umfangreichere Werksammlungen sowie zwei Biografien. (Inzwischen existiert außerdem eine recht beachtliche Anzahl an Nachrufen, Rezensionen; die meisten allerdings aus den 1990er- und frühen 2000er-Jahren.) Inge Müller, so liest man mit leichtem Zucken im Mundwinkel, darf heute zum »gesamtdeutschen Literaturkanon« gezählt werden. Und dass, obwohl ihr literarisches Werk vergleichsweise überschaubar geblieben ist: Im Nachlass finden sich an die dreihundert Gedichte, einzelne, eher prosaische Kurzerzählungen, ein Romanfragment namens »Jona« sowie unzählige undatierte Typo- und Manuskripte, lose Zettel, deren Urheber aufgrund der symbiotischen Arbeitsweise des Ehepaares (auch hinsichtlich der frühen Theaterstücke Heiner Müllers) manchmal nicht ganz klar auszumachen ist. Das mitunter Rätselhafte nach der Frage der Autorenschaft mag zu einer Mythisierung der hinterlassenen Stoffe verleiten, doch nach einiger Durchsicht und Recherche scheint klar zu sein: Was damals aus den Nachlässen Heiner Müllers ans Licht gehoben wurde und heute als eigenständiger Inge Müller-Bestand in den Archiven der Akademie der Künste in Berlin existiert, ist mit der 108-seitigen Auswahl des genannten Gedichtbands *Wenn ich schon sterben muss* materiell sowie optisch bereits bestens eingefasst. (Buchtitel und Name der Autorin prangen hierauf in einer Blindprägung, verschwinden geschmackvoll im kalkweißen Leineneinband. Die Texte sind in kräftiger Bodoni Antiqua gesetzt und chronologisch in Form einer »lyrischen Autobiographie«, wie es die Literaturkritikerin Sibylle Cramer damals in *Die Zeit* nannte, angeordnet.) Was bei der ersten Lektüre jedenfalls sofort auffiel, das war das Kantige, Stockende der Verse. Die teilweise arg komprimierten Zeilen kamen meist ohne jeglichen ästhetischen Überbau oder Metaphorik aus, oftmals musste ich sie zwei, drei Mal lesen, um zu ihrer eigenwilligen Grammatik, ihrem Sound vorzudringen. Müllers Sprache – gleichermaßen lakonisch wie zerbrechlich – schien zudem unter einer enormen Last zu stehen – ihr allbestimmendes Thema: die Aufarbeitung traumatischer Kriegserinnerungen.

Im April 1945 gehört Ingeborg Meyer, wie sie damals noch heißt, zu jener letzten Charge, die von der Wehrmacht in die aussichtslose Schlacht gegen die Sowjets geschickt wurde. Dort ist sie zunächst Nachrichtenhelferin bei der Luftwaffe, wird nach einer misslungenen Desertion jedoch an eine Flakgeschützstelle nach Berlin strafversetzt. Hier, inmitten der Straßengefechte im nördlichen Gleimviertel, zwischen ausgebrannten Fassaden, gefallenen Soldaten und Pferdekadavern, wird sie eines Morgens von einem einstürzenden Haus verschüttet und erst nach drei Tagen zusammen mit einem neben ihr ausharrenden Hund gefunden – sie ist damals zwanzig Jahre alt. *»Als ich Wasser holte fiel ein Haus auf mich/Wir haben das Haus getragen/Der vergessene Hund und ich./Fragt mich nicht wie/Ich erinnere mich nicht./Fragt den Hund wie.«* Der Umstand, den Zweiten Weltkrieg in seinen an Sinnlosigkeit und Zerstörungskraft kaum zu überbietenden letzten Wochen und Monaten noch am eigenen Leib miterlebt zu haben, das Dasein unter den Trümmern, die Ohnmacht des Verschüttetseins, dies alles wird zum existenziellen Stoff, der sie im Laufe der nächsten zwei Jahrzehnte nicht mehr loslassen wird. Es sind Erlebnisse, traumatisch-körperliche Einschreibungen, welche sich nur schwer mit sprödem Pragmatismus absichern ließen: »Ich habe immer versucht«, so ihr damaliger Ehemann Heiner Müller, »Vergangenes zu vergessen, vergangen sein zu lassen [...] sonst hätte ich nicht überlebt.« Auch er wurde Ende 1944 noch für den Reichsarbeitsdienst einberufen, hätte dort jedoch »eigentlich keine großen« Berührungen mit dem »Feind« gehabt. Das Glück, einen eher kommoden Krieg durchlebt zu haben, lässt es ihm später wohl zu, in seiner Theaterkunst wesentlich distanzierter mit dem Komplex der NS-Vergangenheit umzugehen. Dort, wo Heiner Müllers Bühnenstücke oftmals eine historische Totale aufreißen, sich ins Explosive, Expressionistische wuchten, scheint in den Texten seiner heimlich im Nebenzimmer schreibenden Ehefrau kein Millimeter Platz mehr zu sein, um von einer objektiven Warte aus agieren zu können: Ihren Gedichten bleibt nur noch die Flucht nach vorne ins Trauma – ohne doppelten Boden oder gar geschichtliche Projektionen. Es scheint, als wäre es genau jene Konfrontation, jene Distanzlosigkeit zur Sprache gewesen, die ihr letzten Endes zum Verhängnis wurde; aus der niemals hätte eine Freiheit erwachsen können.

Als Inge Müller in der Nacht des 1. Juni 1966 tot aufgefunden wurde, da hatte ihr engstes Umfeld bereits acht Jahre an Suizidversuchen – deren Frequenz sich gegen Ende hin wohl nur als verstörend bezeichnen lässt – hinter sich gebracht. Ines Geipel berichtet in *Auf einmal fiel der Himmel um*, dass der Rettungswagen ein ständiger Gast vor dem Haus der Müllers am Kissingenplatz in Pankow gewesen sei. Wolfgang Müller, Heiners zwölf Jahre jüngerer Bruder (mit dem sie zeitweise in eine merkwürdige Affäre verstrickt ist) meint hierzu später: »Immer, wenn ich zu Besuch war, passierte es in aller Regelmäßigkeit einmal, dass wir die Inge entweder vom Balkon ziehen mussten oder im Badezimmer die Tür einschlagen mussten, damit sie dort nicht aus dem Fenster gesprungen ist; oder [dass wir] auf den Gasherd besonders aufpassen mussten.« Ihr jahrelanges Ringen mit dem Tod, das lässt sich heute wohl sagen, war ein leises Zugrundegehen an den psychologischen Spätfolgen des Zweiten Weltkriegs gewesen; an jener »Wucht erlittener Leiden«, wie es bei Hugo von Hofmannsthal heißt. Dass sie es derart lange noch durchgehalten hätte, so konstatierte später ihr Psychiater, bei dem sie sich Ende der 1950er-Jahre kurzzeitig in Behandlung befand, käme »einem Wunder« gleich. Befasst man sich weiter mit den vorliegenden biografischen Stoffen über Inge Müller, so entsteht zudem der Eindruck, es in ihren letzten Jahren mit einem manisch-depressiven, alkoholsüchtigen, unberechenbaren Menschen zu tun gehabt zu haben, der bis zuletzt allerdings nicht von seinen Idealen abzuweichen scheint. Dazu wieder Wolfgang Müller: »Sie wollte die Welt verbessern. Sie wollte es bis zum Ende [...] Ihr Verlangen nach dem guten Menschen hatte etwas Zwanghaftes.«

Wie hätte sich ein Weiterleben mit all jenen Erinnerungen ermöglichen lassen, ohne von ihrer zentnerschweren Last erdrückt zu werden? In ihren Gedichten konnte das Vergangene zwar subjektiv nochmals durchschritten, doch in der Versprachlichung offensichtlich weder gebannt noch überwunden werden – viel zu präsent, zu fotografisch genau müssen die Schrecken der letzten Kriegstage und -wochen ein Jahrzehnt später noch gewesen sein. In knappen Versen durchschreitet sie aufs Neue »feuerspeiende Straßen«, lernt »Tote zu bergen«, sieht »die Welt in Trümmern« und ist schließlich selbst wieder nächtelang unter Schutt und Asche begraben.

Und wachte auf als irgendwo im Herz der Kontinente
Rauch aufstieg aus offenem Meer
Heißer als tausend Sonnen
Kälter als Marmorherz.

Danach geistert sie den ehemals so vertrauten, völlig entstellten Weg »vom Ende der Stadt zum anderen Ende« zum Ort ihrer Kindheit nach Lichtenberg, wo sie in den zerbombten Häuserruinen auch die Eltern finden wird. Beide wird sie tags darauf alleine mit einer Schubkarre begraben. All diese irreversiblen Bilder und Erfahrungen des Schreckens, niemals wirklich begreifbar, sollten eine bittere Einsicht nach sich ziehen – bis zuletzt sieht sie sich als eine zwischen Stein- und Leichenbergen zufällig »Übrig Gebliebene« des Krieges. Es dürfte im Verlauf ihres Lebens wenig Veranlassung gegeben haben, an ihrer Sicht der Dinge noch etwas zu ändern. Vielmehr dürfte sich ihre Erkenntnis, als sie ernsthaft zu schreiben beginnt, noch verfestigt haben, aufgrund der allmählich durchsickernden Gewissheit, einer staatlich-geförderten Amnesie unterworfen zu sein. Ihre lyrischen Versuche kollidierten immer wieder mit einer SED-Politik, die von Beginn an mit rigorosem Stil ein neues kollektives Gedächtnis zu etablieren versuchte; die literarische und somit öffentliche Aufarbeitung individueller Kriegsneurosen passte hierbei – logischer- wie verheerenderweise – nicht ins Bild einer sozialistischen Utopie. (Noch im Jahr 1952 kam Psychiater Friedrich Panse in *Angst und Schreck* zum Schluss, dass »das psychische [Kriegs]Erleben somatische, also organische Vorgänge aktiviert, aber [...] diese störenden Folgen nur vorübergehend und grundsätzlich reversibel sind und keine Dauererscheinungen hinterlassen.« Angebote zu psychiatrischen Behandlungen waren in den Nachkriegsjahren zudem rar, die medizinischen Anlaufstellen aufgrund geschwächter Infrastruktur meist ausgelastet. Der Begriff der Posttraumatischen Belastungsstörung tauchte ganze drei Jahrzehnte später als *Posttraumatic-Stress Disorder* erstmalig auf; in Deutschland wurde dieser als diagnostische Kategorie sogar erst 1991 legitimiert.) Jener quasi naturgegebene Reflex, schuld- und schambehaftete Erinnerung zu tabuisieren, ist ein Phänomen, das sich bis in die Achtzigerjahre hinein wie eine klamme Pferdedecke über das Gedächtnis Gesamtdeutschlands zu legen scheint. Wie sich nur allzu leicht denken lässt, findet insbesondere im Zuge des Gründungsszenarios der DDR eine konkrete öffentliche Auseinandersetzung mit dem Nationalsozialismus kaum bis gar nicht statt. Die jüngste Geschichte sollte verschwiegen, subjektive Brucherfahrungen hermetisch verriegelt werden; es galt der kommunistischen Widerstandskämpfer zu gedenken, nicht etwa den Opfern. Schriftsteller und Schriftstellerinnen hatten somit mehr oder weniger einer politischen Dienstverpflichtung nachzugehen: In der sogenannten Erbauungsliteratur, deren statische, hypermoralische Geschichten vom Wiederaufbau der Gesellschaft in ihrer wirtschaftlichen und menschlichen Form handelten, sollte ein offenkundig starkes sozialistisches Weltbild dargestellt werden – nicht jedoch die Realität einer Ein-Partei-Diktatur mitsamt deren radikaler Fortschrittspropaganda. Was öffentlich erinnert, gesagt und beschrieben werden durfte, stand somit unter strenger staatlicher Kontrolle. Literatur, welche dieser Doktrin nicht Folge leisten wollte, welche ästhetisch widerständig war, welche aufbegehrte, indem sie sich sozusagen ihrem eigenen Gedächtnis bediente, setzte sich der Gefahr aus, unterdrückt, zensiert, namenlos gemacht zu werden. Man spricht rückblickend nicht umsonst von den *blutigen Jahren*, in denen politisch aufsässige Individuen, oftmals aus den willkürlichsten Gründen, mit Haft und Arbeitslager bestraft wurden. Was von ihnen übrig blieb? Manchmal, wie im Fall der jungen, regimekritischen Studentin Edeltraut Eckert, nicht mehr als ein kleines Oktavheftchen voll Beschreibungen karger Seelenlandschaften und einer nie ganz versiegenden Hoffnung. *»Ich weiß nicht viel von mir zu sagen, / Nur dass ich lebe, dass ich bin, / Und alle Wünsche, die mich tragen, / Sind im Verzicht ein Neubeginn.[...] So steh ich wartend unter vielen. / Ich lache mit und bin nicht froh. / Ich hör und seh mich selber spielen. / Mein Herz ist weit, ist anderswo.«*

Inge Müllers produktivste Schaffensphase fiel ab Anfang der 1960er-Jahre in ein Zeitfenster, in dem es unter der sich zu Ende neigenden Ära Walter Ulbrichts zwar so aussah, als würden für Kulturschaffende langfristig bestimmte Lockerungen durchgesetzt – doch erinnern wir uns: Müllers Gedichte waren in ihrer radikalen Innenansicht, in ihrer formalen Härte und Verknappung und auch ihrer eigenwilligen Zeichensetzung in gewisser Hinsicht beispiellos. Wie sollte der auf Zugänglich- und Vermittelbarkeit geeichte DDR-Literaturbetrieb für solch »subjektivistische« Aufarbeitungstexte Verwendung finden? Auch wehte spätestens ab Dezember 1965, initiiert durch Erich Honecker, auf den Plenen des SED-Zentralkomitees plötzlich wieder ein anderer, erheblich schärferer Wind in Bezug auf die fortwährende Liberalisierung des Kulturbetriebs. Ob Müllers Lyrik letzten Endes pauschal als eine ›verhinderte‹ bezeichnet werden kann, ist jedoch fraglich. Siebzehn ihrer Gedichte erschienen kurz vor ihrem Tod noch in der (heute völlig vergriffenen) Anthologie *In diesem besseren Land*, und sogar ein eigener

Gedichtband soll in Planung gewesen sein. Wie es dem Wesen von Literatur allerdings so entspricht, braucht es stets eine Weile, bis publizierte Texte auch tatsächlich in der öffentlichen Wahrnehmung ankommen; im Kontext jener affirmativ-sozialistischen Geisteslandschaft galten viele ihrer Gedichte zudem als unzeitgemäß, ja unerwünscht.

In diesem Zusammenhang kann auch erwähnte Anthologie *In diesem besseren Land* als ein früher Versuch eines literarischen Gegenentwurfes gesehen werden – gnadenlos unterläuft sie mit einer Auswahl durchweg »falscher Texte« (allerdings »richtiger« Autoren und Autorinnen) sowie einem Mangel an erkennbarem »sozialistischen Lebensgefühl« die Erwartungen der Kulturbeauftragten. Dennoch: Trotz neuer drohender Repressalien und der ständigen Angst, mit seinen Texten aufzufliegen, bahnte sich nun das »außerstaatliche Schreiben«, in kleinen verzweigten Rinnsalen im Untergrund, allmählich seinen Weg. Die Sprache begann im Verschlüsselten, zwischen den Zeilen, mittels Metaphern und Chiffren, einen selbstbewussteren, kritischeren Ton anzuschlagen – eine Art zweite Öffentlichkeit entstand; ein paralleler Gedächtnisraum. In diesen leise sich abzeichnenden emanzipatorischen Prozess von Literatur – der obendrein eine Welle der Lyrikbegeisterung, die von der Sowjetunion in die DDR schwappt, mit sich bringt – fällt nun auch das »geglückte Ende« von Inge Müller.

Wurden ihre traumatischen Erinnerungen letztendlich und insgeheim zu *falschen Erinnerungen* verformt? Oder mit den Worten der Kulturwissenschaftlerin Aleida Assmanns gefragt, »wie verhalten sich divergierende Erinnerungen zum Ideal einer einzigen autoritativen historischen Wahrheit?« Hätte ein frühzeitiger Zuspruch ihrer Gedichte sie zum Umdenken bringen können oder wäre geistige Katharsis durch drohende Zensureingriffe letztlich niemals zu erreichen gewesen? Wie hätte ein Abkoppeln jener Vergangenheit aussehen können, ohne diese mit reichlich Wodka und Wein betäuben zu müssen? Womöglich wäre das infernalische Bild beide Eltern mit einem Handwagen inmitten einer Trümmerlandschaft begraben zu haben auch niemals zu bewältigen gewesen. Was hätte angesichts dessen, einen Alltag noch tragen können?

Träume aus Gummi grau oder blau
Blinde Fliegen am Glas
Drückt euch die Nasen platt
Ich hab es satt
Mir tut die Nase weh.
Bis ich durchs Fenster geh
Ohne Träume
Über die Bäume
Mit dem Wind wild und lau
Quer durch den Weltball
Im Haar einer Frau
Irgendeiner die irgendwo geht
Zwischen Stein Stahl und Leibern
Und den Kopf hebt.

Eine Art inneres Exil. Ein Ausnahmezustand, jedoch unheroisch, fragil, apathisch, gegen sich selbst gerichtet. Einer, der darüber hinaus immer weniger von der einstigen Lebenstüchtigkeit zu berichten weiß. Man ist wieder an das Zitat Wolfgang Müllers erinnert, *ihr zwanghaftes Verlangen nach dem Guten im Menschen*. Denn anfänglich steht sie noch mittendrin, gestaltet maßgeblich das Leben um sich herum. In den späten Vierzigerjahren – nachdem sie zu den vielen Trümmerfrauen gehört, die

die Ruinenlandschaft Berlins fraglos zusammentragen und neu errichten – fühlt sie sich wie so viele andere beschwingt durch die neue Sozialismusverheißung, scheint voll aufzugehen in jenem utopisch-flirrenden Gesellschaftsprojekt. Begeistert liest sie Lenin und Marx, glaubt an das Entwicklungspotenzial, wird SED-Mitglied und kurze Zeit später auch Korrespondentin der Kulturabteilung jener Partei. Sie heiratet den Kommunisten und Zirkusdirektor Herbert Schwenkner, der ihr auf einem früheren KPD-Treffen bereits deutliche Avancen macht und sie mit seiner pomadigen Weltgewandtheit und seinen Kontakten zum schillernden Leben Berlins beeindrucken kann. Schwenkner nimmt sie kurze Zeit später auch mit auf große Zirkus-Tournee. Die heiter-opulenten Aufführungen sind gut besucht, ist die Bevölkerung in jenen chaotischen Tagen doch bemüht, mit allen Mitteln wieder so etwas wie Gegenwart und Alltagsroutine einkehren zu lassen. Aus ihrer kurzzeitig angestrebten Karriere als Tiger-Dompteuse wird zwar nichts, doch scheint sie, die Tochter einer Lichtenberger Arbeiterfamilie, Anfang der 1950er-Jahre tatsächlich in der gesellschaftlichen Oberschicht angekommen zu sein. Schwenkner besorgt der kleinen Familie (mitsamt Müller-Sohn Bernd aus überstürzter Nachkriegsehe) bald darauf ein komfortables Haus am Lehnitzsee in einer neu errichteten Waldsiedlung bei Oranienburg. Dort, abseits von Berlin, inmitten der weiten brandenburgischen Landschaft, öffnet sich der Geist und dehnt sich die Zeit – seit Langem, so scheint es, ist sie wieder ganz auf sich selbst zurückgeworfen. Hier entstehen nicht nur frühe Ideen zu einem Romanprojekt (woran sie über zehn Jahre hinweg vergeblich arbeiten wird), sondern auch erste ernsthafte Überlegungen, den Schritt als freie Schriftstellerin zu wagen. Ihre Vergangenheit ist ihr dabei jedoch stets auf den Fersen. *»Ich schrieb und schrieb/Das Grün ins Gras/Mein Weinen/Machte die Erde nicht naß/Mein Lachen/Hat keinen Toten geweckt/In jeder Haut hab ich gesteckt./Jetzt werd ich nicht mehr schrein/Daß ich nicht ersticke am Leisesein!«* Es sind diese knappen, fast in der Art eines Kinderreims endenden Verse, die die beengende Wirklichkeit jener Tage aufzeigen: Was in den ersten Nachkriegsjahren noch in einem nervösen Gemisch aus blinder Euphorie, Liebestaumel und manischem Arbeitsethos übertüncht werden konnte, begann hier in der vermeintlichen Idylle am Lehnitzsee wieder aufzubrechen. Es sind Zeilen, die nicht nur von einer zunehmenden Entfremdung mit dem kommunistischen System sprechen, sondern auch vom beschwerlichen, im Grunde unzumutbaren Übergang zu Normalität und Alltag – eine Bürde, die sie dieser Jahre mit so vielen Kriegsüberlebenden teilt. Dass sie im geräumigen Klinkerbau in Lehnitz zeitweise mit Noch-Ehemann Schwenkner (obere Etage) und Neu-Bekanntschaft Heiner sowie dessen Bruder Wolfgang (untere Etage) in kommunenähnlichen Verhältnissen wohnt, erleichterte ihre Situation vermutlich kaum. (Ob dies ein erster demonstrativer Einspruch gegen die gesellschaftlichen Konventionen mitsamt ihrer starren Sexualmoral war? Wahrscheinlich ließe sich ihre Affäre zum damals noch minderjährigen Wolfgang Müller so ähnlich erklären; weniger grenzüberschreitend macht sie das jedoch nicht). Ihren Brotberuf, das Schreiben von Kinderbüchern oder leichten Revue-Programmen, muss sie derweil auch des öfteren familienintern verteidigen: Heiner Müller gibt in seiner Autobiografie *Krieg ohne Schlacht: Leben in zwei Diktaturen* zu Protokoll: »Ich habe damals den großen Fehler gemacht, ihr zu sagen, was ich [von den Kinderbüchern] hielt. Ich war jung und arrogant. Dann begann ihr großer Kampf, mir zu beweisen, dass sie auch anders

schreiben konnte. Selten hat sie mir etwas davon gezeigt.« Leicht ist zu vermuten, wie beschwerlich ihre Suche nach literarischer Form und individueller Stimme mit einem derart fragilen, ungeheuerlichen Stoff gewesen sein muss. Woher sollte sie wissen, ob das, was sie zu Papier brachte, auch wirklich etwas taugte?

Um die Ecke Urwald hinter Mauern Meere
Zwischen Straßenschildern Laternen und Gewehre
Überm Bahnhof eine Wolke schwarzgrau in Eile
Ein Schornstein schreibt Zeile für Zeile
Chronik der Stadt in den blauen Dunst
Formeln Farbe Schwarze Kunst

So etwas wie Ruhe und Beständigkeit will auch fünfzehn Jahre nach Kriegsende nicht in ihr Leben einkehren.

Man schreibt die frühen Sechziger, die Müllers – mittlerweile verheiratet, beide freischaffend und mit einträglichen Auftragsarbeiten für den Rundfunk einigermaßen abgesichert – sind inzwischen wieder in die Großstadt nach Pankow gezogen, als das lange als DDR-Staatsgeheimnis gehütete Vorhaben, Ost-Berlin einzumauern, plötzlich Realität wird. Chruschtschow und Ulbricht machen ernst: 1961 ist die Grenze dicht, Berlin endgültig gespalten. Obwohl sich zu diesem weltpolitischen Ereignis meist nur Andeutungen in ihren Gedichten finden, muss Inge Müller die Ummauerung sehr wohl, wie Ines Geipel berichtet, als »persönliche Bedrohung und neuerliche Kriegssituation« empfunden haben. (Was in ihrer Vita oft übergangen wird: Bereits Jahre bevor ihrem Gatten, bringt es die ›reisefreudige Ehefrau Heiner Müllers‹, wie es in den Stasi-Unterlagen über sie heißt, auf die Bühnen der gesamten Republik. Mit ihrer Bearbeitung des russischen Theaterstücks *V doroge*, einer nihilistischen Coming-Of-Age-Erzählung, die von individueller Verortung in einem desolaten Nachkriegsrussland handelt, begleitet sie die Besetzung des Gastensembles des Deutschen Theaters nach Frankfurt am Main. Kurz zuvor entsteht zudem das rundum gelungene Hörspiel *Die Weiberbrigade*, das aus gemeinsamen Recherchen des Ehepaares auf dem Areal des Braunkohle-Kraftwerks Schwarze Pumpe resultierte.) Déjà-vu-Erfahrungen unguter Art muss sie im selben Jahr auch verspürt haben, als ihrem Ehemann wegen des provokativen Theaterstücks *Die Umsiedlerin* der Prozess gemacht wird. Ausgehend von Walter Ulbrichts vermeintlich progressivem Appell, die Bühnenstücke hätten nun verstärkt »anti-didaktisch« zu sein, hatte Heiner Müller zuvor ein Stipendium vom Deutschen Theater zugesprochen bekommen. Das Projekt selbst wurde von der DDR-Kulturpolitik zwar gefördert, oblag somit jedoch insgeheim direkter Bindung und Kontrolle. Zwei Jahre konnte er unbehelligt an dem Stück schreiben, konnte, in der Annahme künstlerischer Ungebundenheit, den proletarisch-sozialistischen Stoff nach Belieben formen und dystopisch umkehren. Dass sich die politische Landschaft inzwischen buchstäblich verhärtet hatte, bekam er in seiner bohèmen Zurückgezogenheit anscheinend nicht mit: die Premiere des Stücks im September 1961 überschnitt sich zeitlich genau mit dem Bau der Berliner Mauer, wodurch die Aufführung von den zahlreich anwesenden Kulturbeauftragten plötzlich als »antikommunistisch« und »konterrevolutionär« interpretiert wurde. Mit hart geführter Kampagne ging das Zentralkomitee in Folge gegen das »skandalöse« Bühnenstück vor, beschlagnahmte alle Arbeitsmaterialien und Manuskripte (welche in derselben Nacht von Inge und Heiner noch einmal abgetippt wurden) und setzte es schließlich ab. Für die Müllers, die in jenen Jahren das mythische Ideal eines kongenialen Dichterpärchens am ehesten erfüllen, brechen nun harte Zeiten an. Beide besitzen sie nach der Absetzung der *Umsiedlerin* weder viel an Geld noch an Rücklagen. Die kreative wie ökonomische Stilllegung, so kommentiert Heiner Müller einmal später gewohnt lässig in einem Fernsehinterview, hätten ihn existenziell jedoch nicht sonderlich getroffen, »ich hatte wiederum zwei Jahre Ruhe«, »es war ein Freiraum, auch wenn es aussah wie eine Umzäunung«. Für seine Partnerin – mittlerweile fest verankert im gemeinsamen Arbeitsverhältnis – scheint es jedoch ein Abstieg zu sein. »Es war eine schwierige Zeit, ohne Geld, mit Schulden. Sie litt ungeheuer unter solchen Dingen. Mir machte es nichts aus, asozial zu sein, aber für sie war es das Ende.«, erinnert sich H. Müller weiter.

Nach der Zäsur des Mauerbaus, dem permanenten

Ringen um finanzielle Sicherheit, der fortwährenden Missachtung seitens des Kulturbetriebs (mehrmals bleibt Inge Müller als Co-Autorin unerwähnt), einer mysteriösen, chronischen Krankheit, dem stetig bröckelnden Arbeits- und Liebesverhältnis zu Heiner Müller und der geistig-seelischen Erschöpfung eines immer noch straff getakteten Alltags, sollten die Bruchlinien nun endgültig zusammenlaufen und sich zerstörerisch vermengen. In einem ihrer meist zitierten Gedichte ahnt sie es wahrscheinlich schon: *»Mond Neumond deine Sichel/Mäht unsre Zeit wie Gras/Wir stehn aufrecht im Himmel/Auf dünnem Stundenglas./Der Stern geht seine Wege/Wir suchen unsern Weg/Wenn ich mich niederlege/Geh über mich hinweg.«* Da ist eine Isoliertheit, eine blinde Wut, eine zunehmende innere Einsamkeit, die auch das vermeintliche Fundament ihres Lebens, jene gesellschaftliche Institution der Familie, nicht mehr zu tragen weiß. Im Mai 1966, so berichtet Ines Geipel, schreibt sie ihrem Sohn Bernd noch einen Abschiedsbrief ins Erzgebirge, wo dieser gerade seinen Wehrdienst bei der NVA absolviert. Ungefähr eine Woche später findet Heiner Müller, als er eines Nachts von Freunden nach Hause kommt (in der Schlussphase meidet er immer öfter die gemeinsame Wohnung am Kissingenplatz), seine »vielleicht bewußtlose vielleicht tote Frau« auf dem Küchenboden liegen. »Ich ging zurück in die Küche und stellte den Gasherd ab, [...]dachte, […] an mein Leben mit der Toten bzw. an die verschiedenen Tode, die sie dreizehn Jahre lang gesucht und verfehlt hatte, bis zu der heutigen erfolgreichen Nacht.« Seltsam: geht man den fotografischen Nachlass durch, so stößt man auf viele, ganz viele Bilder aus ihrer letzten Lebensphase, auf denen ihr rundliches Gesicht zu einem ungezwungen wirkenden Lächeln verzogen ist. Auch Schriftsteller Henryk Bereska, der damals als

Übersetzer beim Aufbau-Verlag arbeitet, weiß Jahre später noch von einer »heiteren, starken Frau« zu berichten, »deren Ende mir unverständlich bleibt.«. Und vielleicht, ja, vielleicht hätte sie somit zu Beginn der Siebzigerjahre noch ihren Jona-Roman zu Ende bringen können. Zwar muss man Inge Müllers literarische Versuche im Nachhinein gar nicht überhöhen (im Nachlass finden sich einige etwas steife, von eher reizlosem Alltagsrealismus getragene Kurzerzählungen) oder es für ein weibliches Schreiben vereinnahmen, doch es ist gut vorstellbar, dass ihre Stimme irgendwo zwischen Irmtraud Morgners schnörkelloser Fantastik in *Hochzeit in Konstantinopel*, Brigitte Reimanns großartig überbordendem *Franziska Linkerhand*-Fragment sowie jenseits der Staatsgrenzen sicherlich auch neben Ingeborg Bachmanns *Malina*, ihren Platz, ihre Daseinsberechtigung gefunden hätte. Es bleibt, zu guter Letzt, die Einsicht, dass ihr recht überschaubares Werk irgendwie eine Menge Undurchschaubares enthält, Fragen aufwirft, Kontroverses nicht auslässt. Wie fragmentarisch vieles zudem erscheint, sobald es fokussierter betrachtet wird. Was in einiger Vehemenz bleibt, das ist ihre kompromisslose, vom Zeitgeist verkannte, mit dem Bleistift hart aufs Papier gesetzte Erinnerungslyrik. Von ihr geht auch heute noch ein schwaches Funkeln, eine unbestreitbare Anziehungskraft aus.

Während Inge Müllers Texte bis ins letzte Satzzeichen mit traumatisch Erlebtem aufgeladen sind und kaum noch literarische Kunstgriffe aufweisen können, lässt sich beim Schreiben von Wolfgang Hilbig mehr von einer starken autobiografischen Grundierung sprechen. In seiner Prosa sind die Protagonisten oftmals – ganz klassisch – Projektionsflächen oder Repräsentanten, sind sozusagen Bedingung, um die jeweiligen biografischen Stoffe

aus einer exzentrischen Außenansicht betrachten, bearbeiten zu können. Es sind jedoch nicht weniger Dokumente eines Lebens, in der das Schreiben von zentraler, man möchte meinen, schicksalhafter Bedeutung gewesen war. In beiden Werken lässt sich der innere Bruch mit der kommunistischen Utopie und einem daraus resultierenden Schwellenzustand des Ein- und Ausgeschlossenseins ausmachen.

Es sind dabei diverse DDR-Vergangenheiten und -Repressionsapparate, unter denen sich das freie, nichtideologische Schreiben seinen Weg bahnen musste. Inge Müllers Kriegslyrik hatte – sofern sie denn letzten Endes wirklich gesehen werden sollte – zu ihren Lebzeiten durch eine rigide gesteuerte Gedächtnispolitik kaum eine reelle Aussicht auf Publikation. Wolfgang Hilbig hingegen geriet ab Mitte der Sechzigerjahre, als Honecker bereits regierte, in einen politischen Zeitrahmen, in dem es zwar staatliche Privilegien für den Mittelstand und sogar Privatunternehmer gab (erstmals wurden Steuervergünstigungen und vermehrt Gewerbegenehmigungen verteilt), in dieser der Kulturbetrieb jedoch nicht weniger nach stalinistischem Vorbild gelenkt wurde – im Gegenteil: Hilbigs literarische Versuche hatte man von Beginn an versucht, taktisch zu verhindern. Bis zu seiner Übersiedlung in die Bundesrepublik 1985 wurde er über Jahre hinweg für seine »ideologisch-ästhetischen Verwirrungen« schikaniert, zeitweise auf penibelste Art und Weise überwacht. Bereits Ende der Fünfzigerjahre fiel Hilbig, damals noch Geräteturner, der Staatssicherheit auf. In den Unterlagen wird er zwar in allen sportlichen Angelegenheiten als ›überaus eifrig‹, jedoch ebenso als ›auffällig desinteressiert am Kollektiv‹ beschrieben (beste Voraussetzungen also, um sich dem eher asozialen Prozess des Schreibens zu widmen). Er sollte es in der DDR zu kaum einer nennenswerten Buchveröffentlichung bringen – bei den Kulturbehörden stieß sein literarisches Schaffen mit seinem »nihilistisch-pessimistisches Weltbild«, wie es weiter heißt, immer wieder auf Vorbehalte und Ablehnung (darunter so manch abgeschmetterter Visa-Antrag für Lesereisen in der BRD). Entgegen der öffentlich propagierten Erzählung von künstlerischer Freiheit und Vielfalt existierte offenbar also noch bis in die Schlussphase der DDR hinein eine repressionsgesteuerte Kulturlandschaft. Es scheint, als wäre das Schreiben innerhalb dieses irrwitzigen Spannungsfeldes aus drohenden Zwangsmaßnahmen, Vorladungen oder Zuchthausaufenthalten ein permanentes Ringen um Identität, einer individuellen Sprache gewesen. Eine ständige seelische Gratwanderung, um irgendwann nicht gänzlich dem Wahnsinn zu verfallen.

Eine der großen Gefahren ist es demnach wohl, die Qualität der jeweiligen literarischen Texte, welche ja nichts anderes als ein Protest gegen den Ist-Zustand der Welt gewesen sind, vordergründig nach der Härte des Schicksals seines jeweiligen Urhebers zu bewerten wollen. Trägt die eigene überschaubare Erfahrung, die von existenziellen Einschränkungen und Brucherfahrungen weitestgehend verschont blieb, überhaupt, um über dieses verflixt schwierige Thema schreiben zu können? Die Tatsache, dass die hier versammelten Schriften (und die vieler weiterer observationsgeschädigter Schriftsteller und Schriftstellerinnen) vor der Folie eines quasi-diktatorischen Staates entstanden sind, ist keinesfalls unerheblich. Und doch: Ist diese relativierende Perspektive, diese Hemmnis eines nachgeborenen Westlesers überhaupt nötig? Sind es nicht ganz andere Rezeptionsarten und Aspekte, die diese Texte letztendlich verdienen, die ihnen gebühren? Gilt es nicht der viel simpleren Frage nachzugehen: Was ist uns wirklich nahe, was korreliert mit den eigenen Erinnerungen, Haltungen, ja, Eigenarten? Kann es nicht auch ein kleines Wiederentdecken von Werken von ästhetischem Eigenwert sein?

Betrachtet man das jeweilige Schreiben zunächst an seiner Oberfläche, so lässt sich sagen, dass die Texte von Inge Müller im Vergleich zum artifiziellen Stil Hilbigs sicherlich nicht darauf abzielen, als ›schöngeistige‹ wahrgenommen zu werden. Mehr sind es spröde, minimalistische Gegenwelten, unprätentiös in ihrer Form, die heutzutage jedoch gegenwärtiger sein könnten als manch abgehangener Bestseller aus dieser Zeit. (Natürlich kann es an dieser Stelle nicht um Objektivität oder Vollständigkeit gehen, mehr soll der eigenen Neugierde und des verqueren Geschmacks nachgegangen werden.) So unterschiedlich ihre Lektüre auch sein mag, in beiden

Textkörpern sind sie genauestens modelliert: die inneren Vorgänge des mit allen Eigenarten ausgestatteten Individuums am Rande der Gesellschaft, seines Ichs, seiner Vernunft, und darüber hinaus. Denn beide waren sie geflüchtet: vor den Schrecken des Krieges, vor dem Kommunismus, vor der Enge des Alltags, vor der Staatssicherheit – vor der Vorbestimmung ihres Schicksals. Tatsache ist, dass beide Lebenswege irgendwann einen Knick bekamen, der allmählich zu innerer, wie äußerlicher Heimatlosigkeit führte. Was bedeutet es in einer vermeintlich klassenlosen Gesellschaft zu leben, und dennoch nirgendwo dazuzugehören? Diese Unbehaustheit, dieser seltsame Schwellenzustand ist es darüber hinaus auch, der ihre Werke in einer tieferen Textstruktur vereint. Dass die jeweilige Sprache vor jenem dräuenden Hintergrund nie in abgeklärten Pessimismus, didaktische Alt-Herren-Attitüde oder verbissenen Ost-West-Sprech umschlug, macht sie für meine Begriffe auch heute noch unbedingt lesbar. Durchdrungen von erzählerischer Kraft und ästhetischer Kompromisslosigkeit wird in ihr das Abseitige, das Verborgene, das längst Vergangene, das buchstäblich »Verschüttete« heraufbeschwört – die rückseitige Erzählung eines »realistischen Sozialismus«. Eine, die jedoch nie zum absoluten Gegenmodell gerät, sondern mehr individuelle Erinnerungsarbeit ist, die nebenbei die ganze Gewaltgeschichte und Unterordnungstradition des letzten halben Jahrhunderts gespeichert hat.

II.

Eingebettet in Schwefelgeruch und Asche ist auch das singuläre Werk Wolfgang Hilbigs. Geboren 1941 in

Meuselwitz, einer Industrie-Kleinstadt im nördlichen Thüringen, erinnert er sich in vielen seiner Erzählungen seiner Jugend und Kindheit: vom Erkunden schauriger Orte der zerbombten, scheinbar immergrünen Umgegend seines sächsisch-provinziellen Heimatortes, zwischen Baracken, Ruinen gesprengter Munitionsfabriken und überwucherten Schutthalden. Dies alles lag in unmittelbarer Nähe seines Elternhauses und blieb eindrücklich im Gedächtnis haften. Es sind Landschaften, die ein Leben lang in ihm weitergeistern sollten; Landschaften, die er »im Wissen um die Asche der Toten«, wie Michael Opitz es in seiner Hilbig-Biografie beschriebt, in seinen Texten immer wieder bereisen wird.

Hilbigs obsessives, leider zu kurzes Schreibleben umfasst Unmengen an Lyrik, doch sind es insbesondere seine frühen Erzählungen und Kurzprosa, die mich in schönster Regelmäßigkeit aufs Neue heimsuchen und die hier als Leitfaden dienen sollen. Es sind Texte wie *Idylle* oder *Schläfriges Gras*, wie *Die verlassene Fabrik* oder *Die Zisterne*, die mich von der ersten Zeile an in ihre Formung aus – wie ihr Autor schreiben würde – schimmerndem Dunkel zogen. Beeinflusst durch Weltliterarisches wie ETA Hoffmann, William Faulkner oder Samuel Beckett imaginiert sich Hilbig in vielen seiner Erzählungen von einer zerfurchten thüringischen Nachkriegslandschaft in eine urtümliche Abenteuerwelt hinein. »Erst später ist mir klargeworden«, so Hilbig, »dass diese Industriewelt inmitten von urwaldartigen Braunkohlewäldern Bilder erzeugt«. Seine deutlich von den Naturbeschreibungen romantischer Lyrik beeinflusste Perspektive changiert dabei mit der Vorliebe für das Surreale und Fantastische sowie den Innenansichten des entgrenzten sozialen Wesens seiner Protagonisten, welches die Texte wieder im Realen, im Alltäglichen verankert. Es ist, als erscheine ihre Welt umso befremdlicher, desto luzider der Wahrnehmungszustand des Ich-Erzählers ist. Günter Ullmann, eigenwilliger Dichter und Maler, ebenfalls in einer Arbeiterfamilie im Thüringen der Nachkriegszeit großgeworden, sprach von seiner schriftstellerischen Arbeit als eine Suche nach »metaphysischen Formeln«. Auch Hilbig scheint sich, in einer als trostlos erlebten Gegenwart, um solche außerkörperlichen Zustände zu bemühen. In einem Land, das, wie Ines Geipel einmal schrieb, ohne eine Seelenkunde, ohne Unbewusstes, ohne eine Kultur des Fragens, der Selbstreflexion gewesen war, spürt er schreibend, sich rückerinnernd den »Zeichen der Transzendenz« nach, um noch mal zu Ullmann zu greifen. *Transzendenz* äußert sich in Hilbigs Sprachkosmos mehr als eine Präsenz des Abwesenden. Unter seiner fast halluzinatorisch gesteigerten Betrachtungsweise, jenem »fortwährenden Dämmer meiner Phantasie«, entsteht so aus dem tristen Meuselwitz eine rauschhafte Nachkriegstopografie mit bedrohlich-vibrierendem Eigenleben. Unter dem warmen Gras, auf dem er in den Sommernachmittagen alleine liegt, längs der Pfade am Waldrand, die er in der Abenddämmerung durchstreift, in den Straßen, durch die er tief entfremdet geht, scheinen die schrecklichsten Dinge passiert zu sein. »Ich hörte noch immer das ferne Rollen von Eisenbahnzügen, das mich umzingelte, das ferne, himmelan flackernde Lärmen der wachsenden Unendlichkeit, ein Dröhnen von Eisen, von Flucht und Entfernung zermahlen, und manchmal von Windstößen ausgewischt, und wieder Rollen, rollendes Geräusch, das mein Hasten durch die Müdigkeit unablässig begleitete.«

Ein Großteil seiner Prosa durchzieht diese bildgewaltige, somnambule Sprache. Eine Sprache, in der – sieht man einmal von ihrem geschichtlich-traumatischen Hintergrund ab – nicht zuletzt auch die Leidenschaften einer Kindheit allesamt genauestens beschrieben zu sein scheinen. Oftmals sehe ich bei der Lektüre in eigene, verblichene Bilder der Erinnerung hinein, derart wie es mir bei kaum einem anderen Autor oder Autorin geschieht. Bilder der Verwunderung und Verstörung, die ich im Laufe der Jahre vielleicht vergessen hatte, die absanken und halb reflektiert irgendwo weiterglommen. Dabei lese ich Hilbigs Texte eher unsystematisch, oftmals streife ich in den Abendstunden nur etwas in ihnen herum, setze hier und dort an, erfahre über seinen Arbeitsalltag als Heizer, über die verseuchten, dampfbadartigen Kneipen, die er in seinem unstillbaren Durst regelmäßig aufsucht, über das kalte, »von Nässe überspülte« Leipzig der späten Achtzigerjahre, und gelange stets wieder in die schattenhafte, dunkelgrüne Gedämpftheit vieler seiner Jugend- und Kindheitserinnerungen zurück.

Für Hilbigs Protagonisten ist dieses Grün immer Zuflucht und Grauen zugleich. Zwar ist die Flora rund um das Industriestädtchen, in dem zahlreiche dieser Geschichten angelegt sind, oftmals auf wundersamste und präziseste Weise beschrieben, doch scheint ihre üppige Vielfalt ebenso eine dement wuchernde zu sein; wirkt roh und archaisch. In der Kurzerzählung *Flaschen im Keller* kippt diese Fülle regelrecht ins Absurd-Komische, indem das Obst des heimischen Gartens die Familie des Erzählers in den Nachsommern buchstäblich »überschwemmt«. Die frech vor sich hintreibenden Früchte der Obstbäume sind kaum noch zu bewältigen, scheinen sich jeglicher Kontrolle zu entziehen. In einem Abschnitt heißt es: »Schon die nächste Invasion von Obst [schien] an die Treppenstufen des Hauses zu quellen; längst war das Gehen auf irgendeinem Platz der Wohnung unmöglich geworden, im seifenglatten Matsch auf den Dielen rollten Birnen und Äpfel als Fußfallen, und die Flottenstärke der obstgefüllten Handwagen, Wannen, Wäschekörbe, die den Hof eingenommen hatten, war ins Unübersehbare gewachsen.« Doch nehme man sich in acht vor dem Frühherbst und seiner »brennenden Sonne«, wenn »das Pflaster [auf dem Hof] sich in einen Sumpf von gelber Süße [verwandelte], Honig und Sirup zwischen den sich zersetzenden Wagenbrettern hervor[troffen] und versanken in trägen Bächen in den Gossen.« Nicht unähnlich den makabren Kammerstücken des österreichischen Schriftstellers Thomas Bernhard, flimmert in Hilbigs Werk manchmal eine beißende Ironie unter der Oberfläche, die mich des öfteren schon, wenn auch leicht verunsichert, laut auflachen ließ. Dass seine Geschichten dabei meist einen ökonomisch knappen Umfang besitzen, mag von einigem Vorteil sein, hängt den Sätzen hin und wieder doch etwas Übersättigtes an; ein Zuviel an poetisch ausformulierter Denk- und Schreibkunst, quasi das andere Extrem zur verknappten Sprache einer Inge Müller oder eines Günter Ullmann. Vielleicht ist es daher auch wenig verwunderlich, dass Hilbigs Bücher, trotz wohlwollender bis überschwänglicher Rezensionen, zeitlebends eher auf wenig Nachfrage stießen.

Als Schriftsteller ging er dennoch radikal seinen Weg. Den ästhetischen Vorgaben des Realsozialismus begegnete er stur mit schwarz-surrealer Romantik sowie extremer Ich-Bezogenheit und schien sich auch nach '89 den Erwartungen des nach einem Nachwende-Roman lechzenden Literaturmarktes nicht beugen zu wollen. In seiner 1991 bei S. Fischer erschienenen Erzählung *Alte Abdeckerei* fügt sich sein bisheriges literarisches Schaffen dann in formvollendeter Wucht zusammen: In einer Art nebulösem Bewusstseinszustand berichtet ein jugendlicher Erzähler von einem kleinen Flüsschen, das in unmittelbarer Nähe seines Elternhauses verläuft. In regelmäßigen Abständen entflieht er der Dumpfheit der Wohnung, folgt dem Lauf des Gewässers und gerät dabei in ein Labyrinth aus dunklen, überwucherten Pfaden und fragmentarischer Erinnerung. Diese halb-biografische, knapp hundertseitige Erzählung erzählt dabei nichts Neues, betreibt seine Sprache – mit den ihn ewig umtreibenden Themen, Heimat, Holocaust und Herkunft – stilistisch jedoch auf der absoluten Spitze. Der Text umkreist dabei, wie so oft, die traumatischen Ereignisse, die sich in der Umgegend des seines Geburtsortes während des Zweiten Weltkriegs abgespielt haben. Überall in der Topografie sind sie gespeichert; plastisch in Form von gespenstischen Ruinen, verrottet im Erdreich oder als Signale in der Luft scheinen sie auf seinen Streifzügen seine Wahrnehmung und Sinne heimzusuchen. »Sollte ich sagen, daß ich allein mit einer Stunde verbunden war, die mich wie imaginäres Fell umwuchs, durchdrungen von elektrisierenden Nerven, die jede Faser der dunklen Luft zu sondern wußte.« (Als Hilbig drei Jahre alt war, wurde in unmittelbarer Nähe seines Geburts- und Heimathauses ein KZ-Außenlager errichtet. Meuselwitz war damals ein reges Industriestädtchen mit großer Braunkohleindustrie; auch der florierende Rüstungskonzern HASAG war in jener Gegend ansässig. Frühkindliche Erinnerungen, wie hölzerne Schlurfgeräusche auf dem Asphalt sollten, wie er später wissen wird, von den Sträflingskolonnen des Lagers, welches eine direkte Anbindung zu den Werkhallen des Rüstungskonzerns besaß, herrühren.) *Alte Abdeckerei* will den Erwartungen der bundesrepublikanischen Öffentlichkeit – überraschenderweise – so gar nicht gerecht werden. Statt konkreter Beschreibungen der neuen Lebensumstände, die der Umsturz der DDR mit sich brachte, ergießen sich in dem Büchlein die unbegreiflichsten Sätze: »Alte Ab-

Die ehemalige alte Abdeckerei in den frühen 1990er-Jahren

deckerei, sterngestirner Umfluß. Alte Abdeckerei unter dem Dach ratloser Gedanken, ratloses Geklapper altüberdachter Gedanken, alte Abmacherei. Nachtgedachte Gedanken, gestirnt: altes Abgeklapper, das Gestirn bedeckt. Und Wolken, altes Geräusch: Rauchgehirn hinter Wolkenstirn, windiges Dach von Abgewölkten, das die Sterne deckt. Unten aber der Fische gewundenes Licht: wie Sternenschrift, gewunden und mit sachtem Zirpen aus der Luft gefallen. Vorbei an Winkeln dichtgedrängter Häuser, vorbei an den Straßen, schneller fallend und verschwunden. Im entlichteten Fluß, im versunkenen Fluß, wolkenüberdacht, und schwindend mit den Wassern in die Nacht.« Kurz darauf erschien mit *»Ich«* – bis heute Hilbigs erfolgreichstes Buch – zwar eine Art literarische Abrechnung mit dem Staatssicherheitsdienst, doch sollte er erst im Jahr 2000 mit dem niederschmetternden wie bekenntnisreichen Roman *Das Provisorium*, seine Form des Wenderomans (und gleichzeitig Autobiografie) abliefern.

In diesem Buch ist auch beschrieben, wie ihn der Gedanke an das heimatliche Meuselwitz, nachdem er Mitte der Achtzigerjahre in die Bundesrepublik übersiedelt, immer wieder aufs Neue heimsucht (als ihm die Kulturbehörde in Darmstadt ein Schreibstipendium zuspricht, bekommt er durch tatkräftige Mithilfe einiger Verbündeter wie Christa Wolf oder Franz Fühmann und nach Jahren der sturen Ausdauer tatsächlich ein einjähriges DDR-Dienstvisum gestellt). Hier lebt er, zunächst in Hanau, danach in Nürnberg, in einem merkwürdigen Schwebezustand, der geprägt ist von schwerer Alkoholabhängigkeit, sexuellen wie zwischenmenschlichen Unzulänglichkeiten sowie, letztendlich, einem unergründbaren Selbsthass, der ihn beinah verstummen lässt. Kaum etwas bringt er zu dieser Zeit zu Papier.

Wie gelähmt scheint er in den kahlen Räumen seiner provisorisch eingerichteten Wohnungen zu sitzen, und sieht, durch den trügerischen Schleier seiner Trinksucht, doch immer nur das urwüchsige Idyll Ostthüringens vor sich aufschimmern. Er, der bis dato fast vierzig Jahre in Meuselwitz gelebt hatte und für das »widerliche Schlangennest einer Kleinstadt« am Ende doch nichts als Wut und Sprachlosigkeit übrighatte, bricht, wie von einem Sog geleitet, in regelmäßigen Abständen wieder dorthin auf. Was bedeutete Heimat für ihn? Eine wehmütige Selbsttäuschung? Ein schuldbeladener Zufluchtsort? Der Besuch bei der Mutter? Eine Selbstverständlichkeit. Jenes dumpfe Gefühl einer Abwesenheit von Heimat sollte sich in ihm, laut eigener Aussage, nach der deutsch-deutschen Vereinigung nochmals verstärken. Dieses erste Zuhause, das nach Vorstellung des Philosophen Ernst Bloch als »ein glücklicher Schein durch die Kindheit fließt« und von dem man erst am Lebensende erfährt, was es gewesen ist oder bedeutet hat, schien Hilbig jedenfalls stets ein Unheimliches geblieben zu sein. »Er kam nach Hause, er konnte die Gegend schon riechen, er roch den Sand, den mit Asche vermischten Sand, und das schwefelhaltige Wasser seiner Kindheit, den Rauch in der Luft und den bitteren Geschmack der harten trockenen Pappelblätter, der über die Straße wehte…«

In Helke Misselwitzs Dokumentarfilm *Winter Adé* ist Meuselwitz und seine großen Schlote in einer Einstellung kurz zu sehen: Der in schwarz-weiß gehaltene, überraschend intime DEFA-Film über unerfüllte Sehnsüchte und Hoffnungen tüchtiger, unbeugsamer Frauen wurde 1987 gedreht und zeigt in besagter Szene ein eindringliches Porträt einer Fabrikarbeiterin in einem Brikettwerk vor der Folie eines längst implodierten Realsozialismus. Irgendwo dort auf den rauchspeienden Industrieflächen hatte auch Wolfgang Hilbig einmal malocht. Lange dreißig Jahre war er einzementiert in der DDR-Arbeitswelt, hatte erst als Bohrwerkdreher, Maschinenschlosser, danach als Heizer in den Kellern von Großbetrieben gearbeitet. In der Unterwelt seines Heizungskellers muss in den Siebzigerjahren auch Unmengen an Textmaterial entstanden sein: Hilbigs Lebensrhythmus ließ es zu, bereits einige Stunden vor Nachtschichtbeginn am Arbeitsplatz zu erscheinen und quasi unter selbst auferlegtem Zeitdruck seine »immer gleichen Geschichten« runterzuschreiben, bevor er bis zum Morgengrauen die Öfen mit Kohle speiste. Autor und Literaturkritiker Michael Opitz, der Hilbigs Nachlass sichten konnte, berichtet, dass so manches frühe Notizbüchlein heute noch einen seltsam sauren Geruch jener dichten Atmosphäre im Kesselhaus verströmen würde.

Sein Lebensweg in der Industrie wäre demnach vorgezeichnet gewesen. Gegen nichts und niemand galt es aufzubegehren oder anzukämpfen – außer gegen die eigene Sprach- und Ratlosigkeit. Gegen das Dumpfe, mit sich Eingeschlossene – gegen eine große Einsamkeit, die weite Strecken seines Lebens zu durchwehen scheint. Die Leere der Ausbildungsjahre als Bohrwerksdreher, das völlige Ausbleiben romantischer oder intimer Kontakte. Dagegen der junge, äußerst virile Körper als Geräteturner und Boxer, die mechanisch-repetitiven Wiederholungen beim Training, die Perfektionierung des Muskelgedächtnisses – das Hinauswollen aus seinem ganzen, von Disziplin verklammerten Alltag. Getextet hatte er seit Schultagen, damals noch Western- und Abenteuergeschichten, doch im Verlauf seines Erwachsenwerdens geriet seine »Schwarzarbeit des Schreibens« immer mehr zur radikal subjektiven Innenschau. Sein lyrisches Ich konnte »aus der augenblicklichen Zeit sich wegdenkend«, die

Begebenheiten und Ereignisse, für die er früher noch keine Worte hatte, zum ersten Mal überblicken und schildern – von hier an könne er die Ursache seiner Sprachlosigkeit vielleicht ergründen. Mit seiner »Berufung«, schriftstellerisch aktiv zu werden, geriet er jedoch auch in einen bis zu seiner Übersiedlung andauernden Konflikt mit den Behörden der Staatssicherheit, die Hilbigs Schreibexistenz meist »völlig verständnislos, wenn nicht feindlich« gegenüberstanden. Immer wieder lagen Ablehnungsschreiben in seinem Briefkasten, deren tumbe Begründungen er mit zunehmend flimmernder Wut las. Enttäuscht, demotiviert und von einiger Scham getrieben, verbrannte er daraufhin, so die Legende, einen Großteil seiner Manuskripte. Und auch in der Folgezeit zeigten sich die Behörden wenig kulant gegenüber seinen eigenwilligen, an Romantik und Expressionismus geschulten Texten: 1966 konnten zwar vier seiner Gedichte in *ich schreibe*, einer vom Zentralkomitee für Kulturarbeit initiierten Zeitschrift für schreibaffine Arbeiter abgedruckt werden, doch wurden diese ebenfalls mehr mit einem Naserümpfen beäugt, waren eher publizistische Ausnahmen. Als Autor blieb Hilbig in seinem Heimatland somit überwiegend ein Unbekannter. Seine erste eigenständige Veröffentlichung *abwesenheit*, erschien erst 1979 – exklusiv in der Bundesrepublik. Die in Frankfurt bei S. Fischer veröffentlichte Gedichtsammlung – der renommierte Verlag wird durch einen Rundfunkbeitrag des MDR auf Hilbig aufmerksam – machte ihn in der DDR mit einem Male zum Störfaktor, zum Dorn im Auge der Kulturbeauftragten. Bei der Staatssicherheit war er von nun an als OPK »Literat« bekannt, und sogar einige Wochen Haft und ein Verfahren wegen »Devisenvergehens« trägt ihm das gegen »staatliches Urheberrecht« verstoßende Bändchen ein. Erst 1983 konnten seine rhythmisch freischwingenden Gedichte, mit solider Verspätung und inhaltlich teilweise entschärft, als *Stimme Stimme* in der DDR verlegt werden. Dort sollte es seine einzige Veröffentlichung bleiben.

Nach wie vor scheint es bemerkenswert, ja frappierend, welche subversive Kraft dem Verfassen von Texten zugesprochen werden konnte, wie wenig es an Dissens brauchte, um aufzufallen, um verhindert zu werden. Wie schnell es zu Sanktionierungen, zu »direkten staatlichen Übergriffen«, wie es Kulturwissenschaftler Wolfgang Emmerich nannte, kommen konnte. Wie groß letztlich die Angst der Machtstrukturen gegenüber jenem weit zurückreichenden Gedächtnis der Literatur war. Wie genuin diese an Ideologie und an Politik – und somit auch an die eigene Existenz – gekoppelt war. Je mehr subjektive Erfahrungen und ästhetische Eigenständigkeit sich im Schreiben vorfanden, umso enger zog sich der tatsächliche Lebensraum zusammen, desto härter waren die Eingriffe der Staatssicherheit.

Im Osten ist es die totalitäre Kulturpolitik, in der BRD die grell-kapitalistische Leistungsgesellschaft, die Hilbig befremdete und nicht heimisch werden lässt. Nie scheint er sich als Zugereister in der Bundesrepublik wirklich einrichten zu können, nicht in Hanau, nicht in Nürnberg und auch nicht nach dem Umzug ins pfälzische Edenkoben mit Blick auf die dunkelviolett schimmernden Weinberge. Produktiv ist er in der Pfalz zwar allemal (und auch seine Alkoholexzesse kann er zwischenzeitlich eindämmen), doch wird er zunehmend von einem finsteren Gefühl der Heimatlosigkeit geplagt, das sich in regelmäßigen Abständen in ihm ausleert. Zeitweise will er sogar gar nicht mehr sein. Wie der Ich-Erzähler in *Das Provisorium* resümiert, sei er, also Hilbig, in gewisser Weise immer staatenlos gewesen. *Staatenlos* wie

der Vater seiner damaligen Freundin und späteren Frau, der Schriftstellerin Natascha Wodin, »der in einem Altenheim bei Nürnberg lag, in abwartender Haltung, der kaum noch ein Wort sprach und der nicht mehr aufstehen wollte. Den ganzen Tag las er in der Prawda oder in der Iswestija, oder er starrte gedankenverloren in den grauen deutschen Himmel oder lauschte in das Preßluftgehämmer des deutschen Baulärms unter seinem Fenster [...] Und durch sein abwartendes Gehirn zog die endlose Fläche des Wolgabogens, der schimmernde Strom, den es für ihn nicht mehr gab.« Zweifellos zieht Hilbig hier Parallelen zur eigenen entgrenzten Lebenswelt in der Bundesrepublik der ausgehenden 1980er-Jahre (und der Gedanke an den im Zweiten Weltkrieg verschollenen Vater, der aus den endlosen Weiten des Wolgatals nie zurückkehren sollte, lag hierbei wohl auch nicht mehr fern).

Im Westen wird er zudem immer häufiger mit etwas konfrontiert, von dem er eigentlich dachte, sich freigeschrieben zu haben – seiner Herkunft. Während Lesungen ist man im Publikum des öfteren verwundert über die grobschlächtige Gestalt des Dichters. Er, der *schreibende Arbeiter* mitsamt sächsisch-schaufelndem Dialekt, sympathischer Boxervisage und einer, wie es DDR-Schriftsteller Volker Braun einmal nannte, »sachten, wie auf Grasland äsenden Stimme«, verachtete jenen *Exotenbonus*, der ihm auf seinen Lesereisen zuteilwurde. »Er wußte immer noch nicht genau, wie er diesen Anschlag auf sein Selbst überstanden hatte, ob er ihn überhaupt überstanden hatte, und man wollte ihm noch jetzt einen Bonus dafür erteilen, daß er ›nicht gerade wie ein Schriftsteller aussah‹ (das war der Grundton der Rezensionen, die er im Westen zu lesen bekam), daß er ›nichts Feingliedriges, Durchgeistigtes oder gar Verzärteltes‹ an sich hatte ... Was für eine Rohheit, was für ein Intellektuellenhass! dachte er.

Die Rezensentin, die das geschrieben hatte, konnte freilich nicht wissen, daß er immer noch auf der Flucht war vor jenem Leben, das ihm seine Visage aufgepreßt hatte. Sein bißchen Geist war noch immer auf der Flucht aus den Todeszellen der Industrie; er war noch immer dabei, zu brechen mit einem Leben, in dem man sein Geld durch ehrliche Arbeit verdiente.« Andere suchten nach solchen Zuständen innerer Zerrissenheit, Hilbig hingegen schien ein Leben lang unter ihnen zu leiden. Seine *proletarische* Herkunft war eine Gewissheit, die er stets mit sich zu tragen hatte, die von ihm nicht überschritten werden konnte; erst recht nicht als selbst ernannter Dichter und Schriftsteller. Es ist eine Gewissheit, die bis an sein Lebensende in ihm irrlichtert und die ihm gleichzeitig (scheinbar unerschöpfliche) Quelle für seine einzigartige Prosa gewesen ist. Man gewinnt den Eindruck, das Dasein als Schriftsteller war für ihn gleichermaßen Pein wie auch Bedingung zum Überleben gewesen. Oft begann er erst nach Mitternacht, wenn alles um ihn herum still wurde, in rotweingeschwängerter Konzentration mit der Arbeit am Schreibtisch; die Tage verschlief er meist. »Schreiben«, so Hilbig in einem seiner letzten öffentlichen Interviews »war für mich ein Schutz gegen alle Probleme, die ich so hatte«. Sein, wenn man so will, äußerst entrückter, ganz auf die Literatur fixierter Lebensstil, verschliss dabei so manche Beziehung – nie hielten es seine Partnerinnen sonderlich lange mit ihm aus. Und doch schrieb er in einem fort, selbst, als ihm zum Schluss die Stoffe ausgingen. Zwar ließ ihn das ewige Nachdenken nicht derart entstellt zurück wie den Schweizer Seelenverwandten Robert Walser, der sich an seinem Lebensende »totgebrannt wie ein Ofen« fühlte und, wie W.G. Sebald in *Logis in einem Landhaus* berichtet, manchmal »steif nur in einer Ecke« der Nervenklinik in Herisau stand, doch wird man den Eindruck nicht los, dass die unentrinnbare Zwangshandlung des Schreibens auch an Hilbig seine Spuren hinterließ. Erst spät bekam er hierfür die Anerkennung – 2002 nahm er den hoch renommierten Büchnerpreis entgegen –, doch seine letzten Lebensjahre sollten von einer rapide sich verschlechternden Gesundheit, knapper Rente sowie Tabletten- und Alkoholsucht bestimmt sein. 2007 stirbt er vom Krebs niedergerungen in seiner Zweizimmerwohnung im Prenzlauer Berg. Man mag sich Hilbig in Erinnerung halten, als den einsamen, staunenden Wanderer, der durch die wüsten, doch wundersam erscheinenden Landschaften seiner Erzählungen streift. Dort vergewissert er sich etwas, was jenseits der gedehnten, verformten Zeit, jenseits der Grenzen »seiner Müdigkeit« liegt. Dergestalt wie es, in eine seiner schönsten Passagen, die sich gleich zu Beginn in *Alte Abdeckerei* befindet, den Ich-Erzähler beim Anblick des von alten Kopfweiden überdachten, leuchtenden Flüssleins überkommt: »Und wenn ich anhielt und lauschte, kam es vor, daß ich mich selbst im Innern dieser Überdachung aus Weidengezweig wähnte, und manchmal glaubte ich mitzufließen, schaukelnd unter einem schwarzen Baldachin aus Weidenzweigen, in einer Barke von ätzender Trauer, unergründlich treibend in ziellosen Kreisen, um auf dem Sand ganz anderer Gegenden zu stranden.«

English version available at laerm-publications.com

Inmitten dieser Sommer waren wir Schatten,
die aus Schatten traten, Schritte setzend,
die aus Schritten folgten,
Schritte, die zu Schritten wurden,
und zu Schritten wurden,
und zu Schritten, Schritten...

WOLFGANG HILBIG

I'm only satisfied with my music when
it can bring me to an inner space which
is rich and mostly egoless,
recalling [...] feelings of my childhood.
This is definitely what I can call home for me.

AXEL KYROU, VOX POPULI!

DE LA COHORTE MYSTIQUE

A small memento of French underground formation Vox Populi!

---

by Benedikt Eiden

It seems to me the older you get, the more you perceive casual music listening as acoustic irradiation. Not that music necessarily has to be always something personal, cerebral or meaningful (on the contrary) but even as background noise, it works less and less in my case. I am not speaking of the collective reception of music here, like going to clubs or the like, whose – at best – visceral experience along with the feeling of bass has always been too much of a crucial component in order to perceive it as incidental. It is more about the moments that you spend with yourself. Especially when being at home or on train journeys, it strikes me particularly: there, I sometimes find music even disruptive, detrimental to my mood. When travelling alone, for example, I'd much rather look out the window, sink into meaningless thoughts, maybe read something or watch people, but trying not to flood my head too much with culture. Often an idea of certain music is enough, which I then follow, and which in its absence inevitably wanders in my memory. In this liminal zone, it seems to me, the music of French underground legends Vox Populi! is dwelling. Recurrently their melodies lingered on me. Often, I could not pinpoint their exact source, yet they seemed so familiar that I couldn't tell whether I had heard them just recently or if they were wafting back to me from the shadowy past.

Quite a lot I have listened to their records over the years, sometimes more or less consciously, yet to this day, I wouldn't know where to put it; the only evident thing is they cannot be assigned to any real genre. Driven by an urge for irregularity and spontaneity (aimed at "surprising the listener", with "the total absence of rules", as bandleader Axel Kyrou says), their songs move along a line whose marks are those strange manifestations or things of which one cannot say whether they're advanced ideas or some musical shenanigans. Of course, assuming any work has the potential to resonate with any listener, it is obvious that each person will react differently. The best way to do them justice is to grasp them in their approach, which might go beyond conventional listening habits, as wondrous, naive expressions of a generation that was socialised with the DIY idioms of punk, then overpowered by the radicality of Throbbing Gristle and shortly afterwards discovered *Fourth World Vol. I, Possible Musics* by Jon Hassell & Brian Eno. Not dissimilar to the work of Hassell, their leitmotif seems to be this *imaginary place* (a sense of place, culturally and metaphysically) and the juxtaposition, the overlapping of technology and tradition. Hassell, with his heavily treated trumpet, must have opened a space of possibilities and utopias for lots of left-field musicians, post-punks in the late 1970s, who saw some of their idiosyncrasies as well as tendencies in improvisation and exoticism further legitimised in his records.

Reference points aside, in the end, one is left with the impression that the work of Vox Populi!, from their first minimal wave sketches (including an Ian Curtis vocal impersonator) to their cassette-only psychedelic collages, to their sinister ambient vignettes, to their later more spiritual tones and exotic-pop-funk interludes, remained in some ways a sole fleeting dream texture. Subconscious music; *Aither* music (as their last album is titled). It thereby doesn't really matter if their songs are often sketchy and sometimes ambling along – it's more about the sum of things, the experience (here this worn-out trope seems to fit for once). Beyond that, one element seems to haunt and hover over almost their entire œuvre: the airy-elegiac voice of Mitra, who with her Persian heritage and lyrics in Farsi, which often draw on folklore songs and nursery rhymes, gives the music, at least to my European ears, something completely enraptured. These, if you will, 'non-Western' aspects could hardly be seen here as a bland pastiche in order to 'capture a vibe'; it's a conjuring of the cultural heritage of her home country from the pre-Islamic revolution years: poetry, pop and folk music overlay with the memory of the desolate yet wondrous landscapes of northern Iran. Saturated with childhood memories of, as she states, "Troubadors and nomads crossing the village of my grandparents, the sweetness of a stream bordered by cypress trees, the majestic mountains of Tehran, the Caspian Sea", her vocals are thus invoking a profound emotional depth and intimacy within the listener. It is as if the group imagines itself into a more arcadian scenery, a place of longing perhaps. These, if you will, cyphers of a past life are most beautifully realised in songs like "Kachalestan", "Golpari June" or "Chirine". At this juncture, also German director Edgar Reitz with his extensive *Heimat* trilogy comes to mind. Reitz, who fled from Hunsrück to Munich as a teenager in the early 1950s, explores here a good 30 years later, in a kind of personal memory work, his underlying feeling of nostalgia that periodically struck him. He, who could no longer stay in his first home had to leave the confines to make his own fortune elsewhere. Whether some leave of their own free will or others are forced to leave for political, economic or existential reasons, this place will probably haunt their memories for the rest of their lives.

Vox Populi! was founded in the early 1980s by a Parisian named Axel Kyrou. Kyrou was enlightened before by one of his visits to England. There in the underground clubs of London, one could regularly catch bands like This Heat, 23 Skidoo or SPK, who were busy changing the idea of what a rock band could be through their intuitive, non-musical approach, including improvisations, effects and tape manipulations. Quasi of 'experimental descent' – Kyrou is the son of Mireille Kyrou, an early musique concrète composer, who was part of the legendary GRM (Groupe de Recherche Musicale) in Paris in the late 1950s – these methods must have struck a nerve in him. Back in France, in his rudimentary home studio, he began recording his first tape together with the help of his brother and his mother Mireille called *Introduction À La Théorie De La Subjectivité Relative*. Soon afterwards, this still somewhat uneven minimal wave sound seemed to be enriched when Kyrou met Iranian émigré siblings Mitra and Arach in 1984, who subsequently joined his project on vocals and percussions. As a mainly three-piece band then, they generated a number of smaller releases over the next year, including the cult classic *Myscitismes*, whose traces we can still be found today in post-industrial groups such as Nový Svět, German Army or Brannten Schnüre. Mitra and Arash were also the ones who brought the oriental folk element (and with it, the melancholy) into the mix. Arash played the percussions or the santur. Mitra sang and occasionally played the flute. Axel handled everything else; rhythm box, tape manipulations, field recordings, synthesizer or organ. Over the course of the decade, the three of them, with the help of numerous musicians and friends, thus brought together a variety of cultural backgrounds in often spontaneous studio sessions – creating a (seemingly selfless) conglomerate of imaginary and concrète music.

On its surface one could detect quite a few things: there are reminiscences of the quieter passages in the music of German electronic legends Cluster, of the mystic dubs of UK's African Head Charge circa *Environmental Studies* (without the sub-bass swagger, though), of the lofty tones of early 1980s Popol Vuh (before they further slipped into new age hell) or of some half-remembered Cocteau Twins melodies. And although they were only active for basically a decade, their discography can be a bit unwieldy to browse through, as it's filled with minor releases, compilations, live tapes, splits and re-issues. On *Half Dead Ganja Music*, perhaps their best-known album, the group's work, however, blends in the most seamless and successful way: released in 1987 by German cult label Cthulhu Records, this record remains a surprisingly coherent, atmospherically extremely dense half-hour, relined by a more noctambulant, gothic feel (in the nostalgic, fuzzy sense of Werner Herzog's *Nosferatu*).

After the 1989 release of *Aither*, an oceanic, dark shimmering ambient record with a fair amount of percussion, scattered free jazz saxophone and manipulated field recordings, the idea then gradually fizzled out. Although the band was still moderately active until the mid-nineties, Kyrou reflects in hindsight: “We came up in '91, '92 with an album for which we did not find any label wishing to release it. I believe that, by this time, we were not industrial, experimental enough for our early followers, and not enough upbeat, techno to appeal to a new audience. The arrival of Techno changed a lot of things for post-punk bands like us. This lack of support from the labels also coincided with the band losing most of its regular musicians.” *Aither* should also remain their last full-length until this day. The music they made after this last hurrah – a logic consolidation of their increasingly melodic approach, far removed from the experimental habitus of their earlier days – is indeed hard to imagine next to the hip, acid-laden electronic music of the time, released on Warp or Touch. (Although, in its best moments Vox Populi! has always been surprisingly danceable. Just listen to the slow-brooding, heavy kick of "Tchi Tchi Vox", "Radio Téhéran", or the erratic electro bounce of "Funk Off". Cut Chemist, DJ of the once-celebrated, now almost forgotten rap group Jurassic 5, has even dedicated a whole compilation of the same name, *Cut Chemist Presents Funk Off*, to the group's beat-heavier tracks.)

I think it wasn't until 2007/08, when some of their earlier material was made available on CD for the first time, that Vox Populi! was slowly being recognised and written about again. Over the next ten years, several more compilations followed, providing an overview of their later phase as well as some of their unreleased and non-album material; among, the excellent tranquil pop of *Alternatif Réalisme* or the harsher tracks they recorded for their split-EP with German absurdist collage maestros Hirsche Nicht Aus Sofa.

The fact that many of their recordings were erring on

the shorter side, their methods relatively sparse, could also be the reason the group's work is still eminently listenable today, perhaps even more so than some of the supposed classics from the industrial/cassette underground of the 1980s. For all their melodic tendencies of their later phase, I assume that the music of Vox Populi! never was intended to be particularly profitable; it still seemed far too fleeting and sketchy for the majority to ever keep it in their consciousness long enough to thoroughly grasp and admire it. At its core, they seemed more concerned with the search for something elemental anyway, an *imaginary place*, a childlike joy perhaps. "Avaze Djodayi" from the aforementioned *Myscitismes* is a proper example of that. This dreamy little minimal synth vignette with its soft pounding beat and hazy melody tentatively reminds me of the first musical sound I heard in my childhood – transporting me back into some vague images. Into the diffusing memory of glowing summers and blaring car radios; of holidays in the Mediterranean, in the south of France in the early 1990s, of which I remember nothing but glaring, bright images, luminous, flickering colours, agate blue water and smashed car windows. Through their music Vox Populi! seemingly want to return to this innocent place; a time when there were no thought-out words, no rational dissection, no overlooking reason. They revel in their musical and ideological freedom, in their naivety and nostalgia. Yet, in doing so, they never came across as overly sentimental or dogmatic, but rather suggestive, vibrant, free-flowing. *Vive la cohorte mystique!*

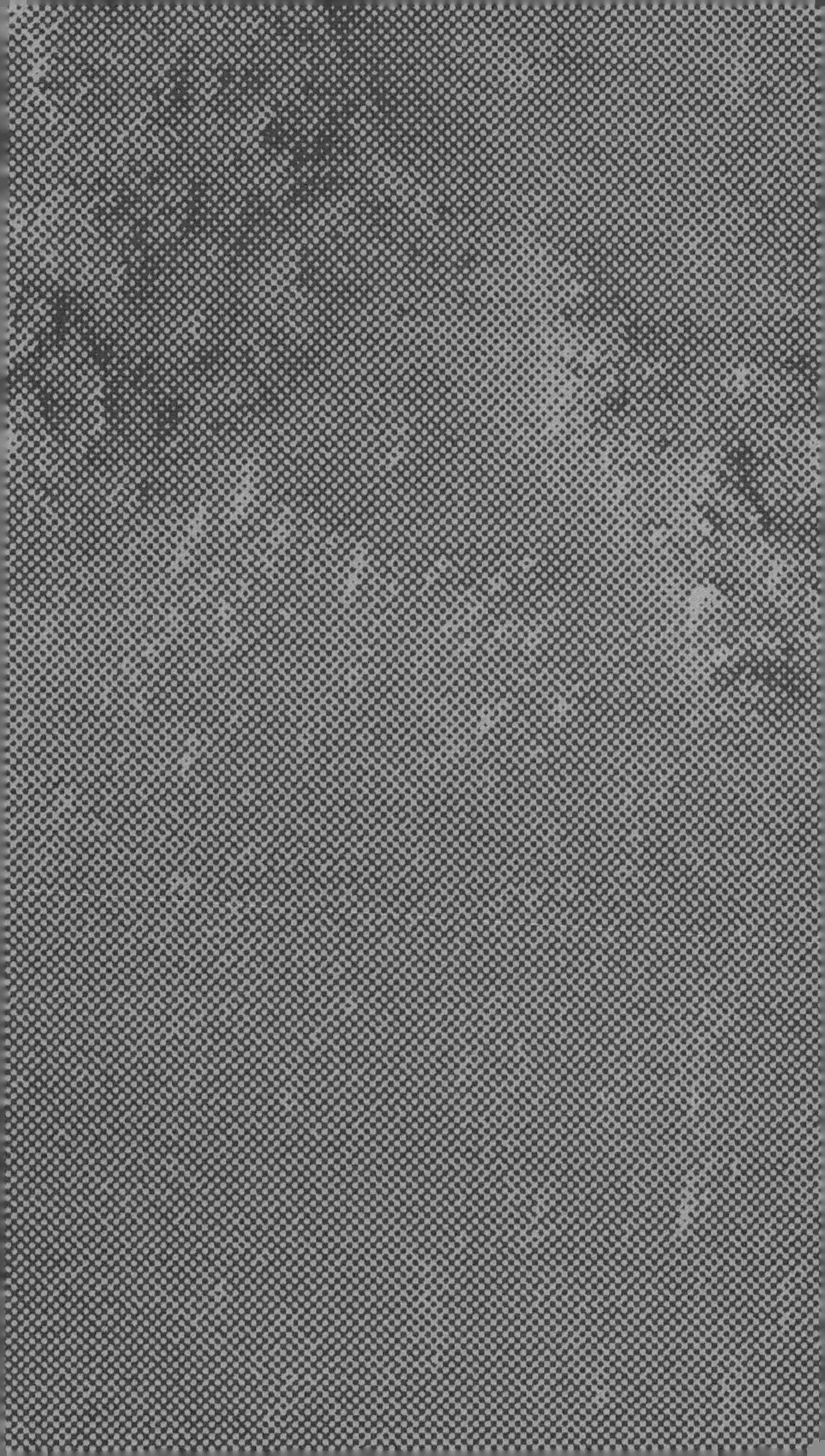

AZUR IN NUCE

Under the spell of Unica Zürn

---

by Lisa Schug

It was the beginning of a love story when the person I dated a few years back introduced me to Unica Zürn and Hans Bellmer in the romantic belief that our meeting was fate – just like Unica and Hans thought when they first met in 1953. Unica saw one of the faces from her visions in Hans and he saw his notorious *doll* in her. Some of the first work I saw of them was a collaboration: pictures Bellmer took of Zürns body parts strangled with a painfully thin thread, like in an SM fantasy. And while Bellmer's obsession with sex just evoked the usual disgust for old horny men in me, Unica sparked my interest. Who was this woman with the characteristic fringe, the obligatory Gauloises in her hand, the stern features and dark eyes that hid nothing? The local library had answers. I sank into her prose, her drawings and anagrams, the literature about her, and at first glance, it swept me away like an ocean wave on a stormy day. I almost drowned in her artwork, her biography, the two lives she was living, her hate-love for Bellmer, the embracing of her own fragile state of mind.

And, to stay with the nautical metaphors, her work

has swept over me again and again in the last couple of years. I've read countless books and articles about Unica Zürn, her life's story and her creative work. This essay is a little journey through all the many facets of Unica's art that never ceases to excite me, that always gives me shivers.

One has to proceed with caution when linking an author's or artist's work to their biography. In the end, understanding art only from a biographical perspective can close more doors than it opens. As in the case of Unica Zürn, however, her work and her life are deeply interwoven to an extent where autobiography and fiction cannot be disentangled.

Born 1916 in Berlin as Nora Berta Ruth Zürn, she grew up in a wealthy yet emotionally unavailable family. Life brought her many hardships: as a child, she suffered enormously from the divorce of her parents and experienced abuse in her own close family. When her marriage failed many years later, she would lose her two children in a custody battle. Many describe this divorce as the end of her first bourgeois life. The later relationship to Hans Bellmer, as I can only conclude from what I read, would nowadays be most likely defined as highly toxic, co-dependent and abusive. Bellmer might have been the strongest advocate of her work and talent, yet at the same time, he brought terror upon her. Alexander Koval, publisher, essayist and long-time friend of Zürn concludes in his notes about the couple, that it was Bellmer who sparked Unica's long term mental distress. No matter how many résumés I read about her short life, the dominant tone is always a grim one. Her writing however was not always as dark. Before she moved in with Bellmer in a Paris hotel room just a few months after meeting him, Unica wrote novels and radio plays for children under the umbrella of *Unica Zürn erzählt* (Unica Zürn narrates) that later aired on Berlin's RIAS (Radio in the American Sector). One of them, to be found in the estate of the aforementioned Alexander Koval, tells the story of two houses that move into the woods, because they cannot deal with humanity any longer (sic!). Her style in these Berlin times has something playfully surreal yet always light-hearted about it.

That changed quite significantly after her move to Paris when she created her most distinctive pieces – a somewhat wondrous but affirmative tone became abysmal darkness. "Und wenn sie nicht gestorben sind" is a striking example of her work in the 1950s, symbiotically intertwining her meanderingly detailed sketches and her disturbingly beautiful anagrams.

Ich bin dein, sonst rennt es weg und
wischt uns in den Tod. Singe, brenne
Sonne, stirb nicht, singe, wende und
geboren, wenden und ins Nichts ist
nie. Entschwundenes gibt Sinn - oder
nicht gestorben sind sie und wenn
und wenn gestorben - sind sie nicht.

("Und wenn sie nicht gestorben sind", 1956)

Impossible to translate, the anagram roughly centres around ideas of dying, vanishing and a burning sun while the drawing displays a monstrous figure – at least that is what I see in it. Four or more limbs are just recognisable while two red eyes look at us from the centre of the picture and it seems as if the figure is giving birth to something egg-shaped. You can immerse yourself in its mutating details that look like straight out of an intense nightmare. What is so fascinating to me about this and many other of her drawings, novels and poems is this pitch darkness, the thick black curtain that lies on her work and never lifts. If it wasn't for the letters Unica exchanged with Alexander Koval and others in which she talks about everyday life and in which one might even sense a little bit of self-irony here and there, one might have asked oneself if this curtain covered her as a whole.

Now, to get a deeper feeling for "Und wenn sie nicht gestorben sind", bear in mind that Unica did in many ways see herself more as a vehicle for an unknown mysterious force that would make her draw and write, inspired by the automated drawings of the surrealists. She often sat at her desk, waiting for the spirit that would guide her – or, as the surrealists would say, for the subconscious to appear. Her sketches and drawings vary from almost childlike scribbles to incredibly detailed gazes into the void. Her anagrams, an inexhaustible pleasure ("unerschöpfliches Vergnügen") to her, often begin with a starting line from the work of French poet and painter Henry Michaux in whom she thought to see her *Man in Jasmin* (yet another figure of her visions and the title of one of her novels) when she first met him. Anagrams, in a way, were like a puzzle to her. Rather than being oriented towards lyrical or aesthetic pleasure, Unica was on the hunt for hidden messages. Legend has it that she yelled out loud when she realized the family name of her friend Max Ernst had the anagram 'Stern' (Star) in it. Other messages were hidden in numbers that had a spiritual meaning to her – 6 as the number of creation and death, 9 as the number of angels and fate. Checksums became an obsession at one point. And while for Unica these hidden messages and her creative input came out of another

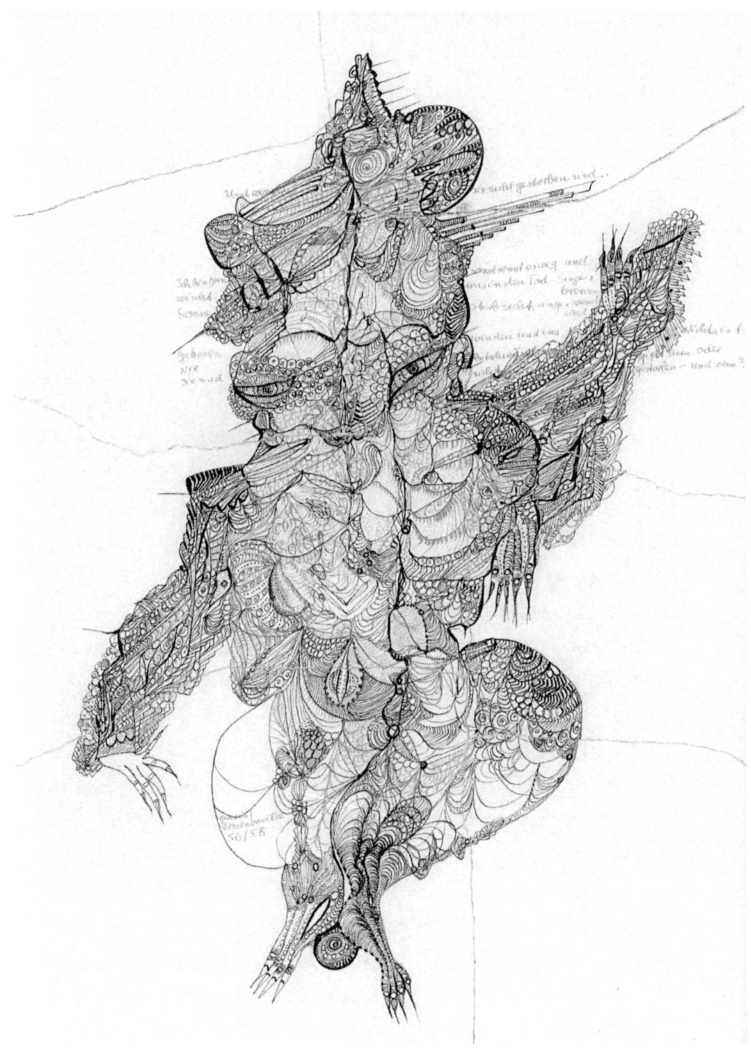
sie nicht gestorben sind..
uns in den Tod
geboren
gestorben – und wann?
56/58

dimension, to me it seems like her pictures, drawings and writings opened a gateway to her soul – to the beings, the structures and the horror that could be found there. This is certainly one of the things about her work that never ceases to amaze me; any drawing is a view right into her naked mind.

Sometimes that aura of loneliness and despair lingering around her work was directly feeding from her life experience. The relationship with Bellmer yielded several pregnancies (birth-control being banned in France by that time), that she decided to terminate after he announced that he "wouldn't being able to resist incest with his [future] daughters". Abortions were criminalized in both France and Germany by that time, so Unica's only way was to undergo illegal, unsafe and traumatic abortions. One of them went so wrong, she had to travel all the way from Paris to Berlin to see a doctor that would be able to help her. It is impossible not to notice how these episodes of unwanted pregnancy are mirrored in Unica's 1968 novel *The Trumpets of Jericho*. The protagonist immerses herself in violent fantasies against a parasitic fetus: "I have a pair of bright and sharp scissors with which I will cut the umbilical cord. Sharp and bright scissors that will be very happy to cut the tender knuckles of the tiny fingers."

To some extent, her work certainly also reflects the mental distress she went through. In her lifetime that meant spending many months, sometimes even years in a psychiatric ward. Unica was diagnosed with 'schizophrenia' and 'nervous depression' or in her words "the beautiful but also sad madness". As long as her visions weren't too strong or violent, Unica did not struggle with or fight against them. She embraced them to a point where she herself confessed she loved seeing things others could not perceive, having a supernatural connection to the world.

Like her protagonist in the *Trumpets of Jericho* says, "Why can't I always live in a state of hallucination? I complain about being bitterly normal for most of the year." Alexander Koval however, deeply concerned with his long-time friend rather sees Unica's need to get away from Bellmer as one of the main causes for her hospitalisations.

Unica, the one and only. A curious thing is that her talent was acknowledged during her lifetime yet forgotten after. She sold her artworks (even at significantly lower prices than her male colleagues), she had exhibitions together with Bellmer as well as solo shows. Her first solo exhibition had André Breton, Man Ray, Hans Arp and Victor Brauner on the guest list. Man Ray took her portrait, Henry Michaux brought her sketching paper to the hospital. Max Ernst compared her to Hölderlin, one of Germany's most famous poets. She was a part of the *Exposition Internationale du Surréalisme* and *documenta II* in 1959 and yet, even if Max Ernst once called her the "greatest (woman) poet alive" and Oskar Pastior dedicated an anagram of her own name to her: "azur in nuce" (azure in a nutshell), it is only 30 years after her death that her art is exhibited again, that people really start discovering her work and today even call her an icon of surrealism. For many years after her death Unica Zürn was forgotten, degraded to the status of 'Bellmer's mentally ill late partner' and it was indeed Bellmer himself who kept and archived most of the work of 'Frau von Bellmer' (Bellmer's woman) as she used to sign her letters sometimes (being sarcastic or fatalist, one does not know).

When tracing the thread back to the question of why a woman with this incredible body of work was in her time and especially after mostly recognized in relation to Hans Bellmer, that thread leads to an ancient structure of sexism in the art world. It also leads us to double standards. Why were Henry Michaux or Hans Bellmer, men whose art was just as clearly shaped by their mental experiences, celebrated artists, but Unica mostly recognised as a woman in distress? If the Paris surrealist circles even had their 'own' psychiatrist, why was she the one that was labelled 'mentally ill' and her work thus devalued? And, let's just think about it for a second: what if some people do indeed have a connection to higher consciousnesses or other dimensions? Think about Swedish proto-abstract painter Hilma af Klint, who also used automatic drawings to record messages that she received from beings of higher consciousness in a state of trance, as she later recalled. What if this applies to Unica as well: channelling figures and ideas from another world or even foreseeing the future.

Sie steigt auf das Fensterbrett, hält sich an der Schnur des Fensterladens fest und betrachtet noch einmal ihr schattenhaftes Bild im Spiegel. Sie findet sich reizend und eine Spur von Bedauern mischt sich in ihre Entschlossenheit. ‚Vorbei', sagt sie leise und fühlt sich schon tot, ehe sie mit ihren Füßen das Fensterbrett verläßt. Sie fällt auf den Kopf und bricht sich den Hals. Ihr kleiner Körper liegt seltsam verzerrt im Gras. Der erste, der sie findet, ist der Hund. Er steckt den Kopf Zwischen ihre Beine und beginnt sie zu lecken. Als sie sich gar nicht bewegt, beginnt er leise zu winseln und legt sich neben sie ins Gras.

"She climbs onto the window sill, holds on to the cord of the shutter and looks once more at her shadowy image in the mirror. She finds herself lovely and a trace of regret mingles with her determination. 'Gone', she says softly, feeling dead even before her feet leave the window sill. She falls on her head and breaks her neck. Her small body lies strangely distorted in the grass. The first to find her is the dog. He puts his head between her legs and begins to lick her. When she doesn't move at all, he begins to whimper softly and lies down next to her on the grass."

Unica writes these words in her novel *Dark Spring* – and this is where the borders and boundaries of fiction and reality finally collapse. In autumn 1970, preceded by a long stay in psychiatric ward, Unica has to move in back with Bellmer in order to to be discharged. What happened then after, we don't know exactly. Some say the couple had their final breakup. Others say Bellmer threatened to send Unica back to Berlin. On the 19th of October 1970, Unica Zürn jumped out of the living room window and died. What other death could she have chosen after writing down her own fate in this book?

FEVER DREAM TEXTURES

Approaching the music of Antediluvian

---

by Benedikt Eiden

Recently, in the course of my continuing admiration, while thinking and researching about the work of Canadian death metal band Antediluvian, I came across a sentence from an interview with drummer Mars Sekhmet in which she states that her band shared a common interest in exploring the *unconscious mind* and what it would mean to be a pure biological mass that has not changed fundamentally since ancient times. Now, while these statements in of themselves may not be particularly spectacular or significant for a genre that tends to draw from the primordial and mythological anyway – it somehow stayed in my mind, attracted my attention. Perhaps this is because with the author of these lines, despite all the tendency towards the rational and tangible, all the alleged enlightenment, there is still a residue for the mystical and metaphysical, which is sometimes being evoked. To then continue on this nebulously naive vibration – one could say that the duo's ambition is to explore the *eternal aspects* of the psyche and body, of the mental and the carnal; a venturing into the remotest corners of the subconscious; the deepest, most veiled past.

Now, if you go by psychoanalysis, dreams are the most direct path to the unconscious. Apart from divergent understandings of modern neurobiology, which fairly say that the dream theory of psychoanalysis, in other words, the symbolic transformation of forbidden desires from the unconscious, is obsolete, indulging in this mythically and symbolically charged sphere seems to represent a way of approaching the hermetic sound wall of Antediluvian. As Swiss psychiatrist C.G. Jung emphasised in *Man and His Symbols*, the dream and the myth are closely connected: "The dream takes us back to distant states of human culture (...) The same desires and instincts are inherent in all people and all nations, which in turn leads to the analogies between the various mythological materials. The dream is the means to open up these mythological contents or the sublimated desires of humanity. It is the expression of the myth." In Sigmund Freud's *Konstruktionen in der Analyse* there is a dream description by Jung in which he uses a spatial metaphor to describe his descent from *personal* memory to an *archaic* one. Therein he finds himself in a house, in which he gradually descends to ever deeper floors. From the living room on the upper floor, equipped with Rococo furniture, he enters medieval rooms on the first floor, then a cellar from Roman times and finally a pre-historic cave. If one would attribute something like a 'dream ego' to the musical entity that is Antediluvian, then it would be located somewhere there, in the depths of an "unconscious mythology", as Jung calls it (likewise, just as all humans inherit similar biology, Jung uses the term *archetypes* to refer to the shared architecture of the psyche.) The band's interest and aspiration in exploring the unconscious mind could thus also be associated with the work of the *archaeologist of the soul* – the, if you will, more passive part of psychoanalysis. An exploration of an archaic memory, not necessarily one of personal nature, but one that reaches deep into the centuries. A memory that, after all, represents man in a state of derangement – a superbly strange world of distant calls from the liminal regions of consciousness, where everything intermingles chaotically. Haasiophis, creative head of Antediluvian, summarizes the group's works as a "research beyond the edges of the boundaries in human consciousness, history and religious studies."

My first encounter with the self-proclaimed "Psychedelic Commando" dates back a good ten years now, and I still remember the sheer astonishment when I put *Through The Cervix Of Hawaah* into the CD (!) player. My appreciation of the band and their music has not been changed by my numerous musical discoveries and shifts in interests. With the same enthusiasm, I still listen to their primitive, clearly Ross Bay Cult-influenced records as well as their later, more complex, cerebral ones.

Their ability to actually make death metal sound like an archaic and perverse entity, in a genre that despite – or because of – progressive refinements and countless aesthetic carve-outs somehow feels as hollowed out and dull in 2021 as it did in the early noughties, is a unique skill – not appreciated by everyone. I vividly remember irritated voices in metal media claiming their music sounded like a "cacophonic flood" where everything would resemble more or less an "overflowing mush". These, strangely accurate attributions might not only be due to their leanings towards the chaotic and atonal, their hypnotically bent, sometimes lo-fi productions, but especially due to the rather unorthodox style of drumming, one might think (as stated in an interview, Mars Sekhmet only started playing and practising at the time the band was founded in 2006.) Admittedly, their style may not be the cleanest, most virtuosic or technical: it feels ritually chaotic, disjointed and seems to be more naturally interested in a distinctive sonic aesthetic with its muffled, tom-heavy and bone-dry thump – sometimes evoking Chris Reifert's reckless pounding on *Mental Funeral*. In general, Antediluvian's music, in its slower, less chaotic moments, seems very much influenced by Autopsy. And just like in their case, you can practically feel, smell and absorb the sound with your senses. Even the vocals sporadically appear as if they are coagulating in something bubbling, fizzling, seem to be *just another instrument* at first.

And in between, repeatedly, moments of retreat: in mostly economically short Ambient passages the 'descent into time' seems to have been stopped for a brief stretch... *"The milk of the stars/Gazing nightside eyes/As the form reduces ashen/Particles return/Consciousness is thrust beyond"* ...Until eventually, the instruments reassemble with incredible power, as the music morphs back into a transparent, murky creature, amoebic, jelly-like, increasingly primitive, blind, smaller as if it could track the path of history. (*Primitive* also seems to be the leitmotif here as it, first of all, leads us to their band name; *Antediluvian* means "extremely primitive or outmoded" as well as "relating to the period before the flood described in the Bible.")

The flow of words and thoughts
Encase reality
The birth of God
Breathing...in, out
Cognizance of being
But for an untimely moment
We reach back for that
Which preceded all thought and form

Then return
To the firmament
Bend, transcend, pushing, throbbing.
Through fleeting external husk
Exegesis of God before men: the awareness passes on
An imposer granting the gift to impose...
Cyclic revelation
Mirror of Orion glows above

It says in "Homunculus Daimon-Eon (Awakening)", the first song on their quasi-masterpiece *λόγος* (Logos). In the same way in which myth and dream are closely connected, so is the former obviously with religion, its discourse and symbols. True to the arts, the seemingly boring science of nature is replaced here by metaphysics and Gnostic worldview. The Gnostic idea of dualism – in the metaphysical notion of an invisible, weightless second body – can be found from time to time in their lyrics. Similar to the ideals of, for example, the Romantic period, the concept of a soul shall lead here to a divine trans-individual core, to a non-self. "*Toward the summit/ The grand ascendance/To a 'throne above the stars of God'/ White hands outstretched/Guided by oracular vision...*". On the way to a possible realm of light above the stars, however, everything is still entangled in a Gnostic drama of carnal alienation – a constant battle of remembering and forgetting, of torment and salvation, of life and death. "*Is all gnosis/The spew of the exiled ones?/A willingness to all influences/Will allow the opener/to taste delight/of decrepit decay/To envision duality/Is to embrace it/To bind with it is to cannibalize/Ones self in empty bliss*". The glimmer of biblical eschatology runs through their lyrics, as well as various mythical scenarios of cosmic chaos. Their interest in (Christian) religion, though, as typical for the genre, is primarily in its corruptive power and the Apocrypha and sectarian speculations embedded in it. Haasiophis again in his own words in an interview with *Voices From The Dark Side*:"[...]I am fascinated by the descriptions in not just the bible but also in apocryphal texts and many other writings describing the tales of these 'supernatural' beings, and with how external opposers have been blamed through history.[...]Regardless of their origin, however, antediluvian myths and cycles often attempt to describe our race's origin in light of a struggle between internal and external influence. We are very interested in how inversion occurs and how the internal and external can mirror each other."

Speaking of lyrics. What brave, even daring undertaking it can be to seriously engage with most lyrical performances in the more esoteric realm of extreme metal, where the tendency to fall for bold, cosmic kitsch always seems just a step away. Antediluvian avoid such tastelessness typical for bands composing overly long, pseudo-epic songs with "dollar-store Pink Floyd jam sections" (to quote Berlin heavy metal institution Radu Baltag) or who getting tangled up in ideological orientations in the form of neo-pagan nature-religion or so-called 'anti-cosmic satanism'. Their lyrics seem to draw their influence more from theopoetic writings and the radicalised, obscene form of sexuality to be found in the works of French philosopher Georges Bataille. Combined with a deep admiration for the musical work of bestial hordes like Beherit or Axis of Advance, their output thus possesses, in my opinion, a psychological sensibility and profundity rarely equalled in modern forms of extreme metal music; perhaps only by the warped horror of Portal or the cosmic violence of Nuclearhammer (even Grave Miasma, for all their abilities, come off as sterile, machist bombast in comparison). Admittedly, song titles like "Sadomaniacal Katabasis (Last Fuck of The Dying)" or "Obscene Pornography Manifests in the Divine Universal Consciousness" may sound as wacky as they are funny, yet they fit well in the context of a (fever) dream sphere with all its blunt libidinous dimensions.

Now, one could, of course, categorically reject all this or call it 'esoteric nonsense'. Ultimately, it is, as often, all a matter of taste. Psychosexual, ancient or cosmic themes and motives aside – all this acts a pleasant superstructure but is ultimately not decisive. Either the music affects you or not. Either you have fun with it, or you don't – *fun*, goddamnit! Just as one can also simply be entertained by the (surprisingly poetic) lyrics – beyond a sphere of sensemaking.

That leaves, ultimately, the visual element, their stunning artwork that creates a raw, mythical iconography. In essence, their work would not be regarded the same way if it wasn't for those mainly copper plate etchings by Haasiophis, a more detailed technical description of which would probably exceed the scope here and basically deserve an dedicated treatise. His art is an endeavour that seemingly allows no more dividing lines between what is commonly called the human and a creature torn out of its natural context. It lucidly illustrates, above all, the biological and the creaturely material layer in their work. Executed with ink wash, acrylic paint, watercolour and the already mentioned etchings, these images reveal a gap between realism and abstraction, between the photographic and the painterly. Furthermore, they somehow remind of microscopic pictures of ancient forms of reproduction, in which bacteria transfer pieces of their genetic material through fine tubes, as well as animal paintings from the older stone age, which were found deep in caves in the south of France. They too were, so to speak, engraved into the material. They too reflect the light to a time when there was probably no such developed consciousness and language as we apprehend it today, no morals.

What shock and strange sensation must have struck those three French geologists in December of 1994 when they unknowingly entered the sites where time had been preserved for thousands upon thousands of years. And outside the cave, on the way back through the vineyards, the hidden, primordial world may have had already become the feverish stuff of their dreams. Speaking of which...

* * *

"A lizard lay motionless in the sun. Some wasps flew out of a hole in the ground and buzzed around fallen fruit. Weak wind passed through the branches of a cedar, and also some metre-high juniper and mallow plants swayed slowly in the midday heat. A strong balsamic scent was in the air. At first, he heard the current; it was a calm, steady rushing. The high-standing sun must have woken him; blinkingly, he looked around. In front of his eyelids waved a glaring veil of desaturated colours. Seamlessly they were lining up, pulsating in his skull, flooding his receptors. The day was of such brightness that he had rarely experienced before. Little by little, the place began to take shape. On the ground, some figs lay scattered, and he noticed a few shards of clay, whose oddly conscious arrangement gave the impression of a deliberately laid mosaic. Twigs hung down with deep green, finely sawn leaves, in between which amber-coloured fruits glowed – everything grew and blossomed like mad, and the stranger suddenly felt a strong urge to feast on this abundance without restraint. But almost like following an eternal order, it first drifted him down to the water. Walking seemed strangely effortless and time-lapsed to him, like sliding through dense atmosphere. Immediately he found himself by the river which, as the stranger now assumed, was meandering somewhere deep from the millennia. Self-forgotten, he looked at the opal-like shimmering water, of which he could not tell whether it was flowing fast or slow. With eyes half strained, he then tried to see behind its reflective surface: catfish, perch and eel seemed to glide around weightlessly down there, observed him with a staring gaze as if they knew some things better. After some time – it could as well have been several hours or days – the stranger started to notice something on the ground that resembled thick smoke, as it usually shoots in pitch-black columns from mineral tubes at the bottom of the seas. Gradually, the smoke transformed into scheme-like forms, until he thought to see images of faces in it; faces he was suddenly convinced he had recognized. Bruised, bearded faces, with vile cuts, wide-open mouths and hollow staring eyes. For a moment they remained stuck in the fibrous river grass, were distorted spookily as if they were made of tough quicksilver, before disappearing again from his field of vision and into the darkness of the current. Escape and rescue impulses were now beginning to chaotically mingle in his head. A feeling, in which the fear of a dark premonition lay, was emptying itself in him until all sensations and over-lappings slowly fell silent. Soon, also the current was no longer to be heard – quiet and deceptive it glided along. Westward on the horizon, suddenly, a storm wall rose; its blackness pervaded by a gruesome blood-red flare. Then, a dull, tremendous thunder was heard, as waves roared through the air. The stranger still remembered being underwater himself in the next moment, slowly descending into a shadowy landscape. In a state in which alive and dead, awake and asleep, fire and water seemed somehow similar, the stranger sank, for what appeared to be an eternity, into the furthest image of himself."

(Funny dream, Sablières, France, 19.08.2019)

Niemand kann sich ähnlich sehen. Er tut es entweder nur im Bild oder nur als Leichnam.

HANS BELTING

WASSER AUS UNBEKANNTER QUELLE

von Tim Nagel

Ich habe versucht, mich zu überlisten. Kurz nach dem ich die Grüne Trift erreicht hatte, rief ich mir die Grenzstriche auf Karten ins Gedächtnis, die Dorf von Dorf, Ortsteil von Ortsteil und Stadt von Stadt abgrenzen. Ich dachte an die kleinen schematischen Zeichnungen auf einer alten Legende der Kartografie, die mir vor einiger Zeit in die Hände fiel: Ziergärten, Weingärten und Hopfengärten, Sand- und Schottergruben, Tabakbaugebiete, nasse Wiesen, trockene Wiesen, Wiesen mit Obstbäumen, gemischte Wälder, Gestrippe, Torfstiche und Meerwassersalinen. Öden und nackte Felsen wurden ohne Illustration nur mit Abkürzungen gekennzeichnet. Zu meiner Rechten, in mittlerer Entfernung, erkannte ich in der Dämmerung ein für diese Gegend außergewöhnlich hügeliges Feld, unbebaut. Ich stellte mir vor, was es kennzeichnen könnte, und entschied mich für Buchstaben einer Schriftart der *Kursivschrift™ Schriftfamilie*, entworfen von German Cartographic Design, die bis Mitte der Sechzigerjahre auf den meisten alten Karten zu finden ist. Schwebend, von unterschiedlicher Opazität, manchmal etwas in die Tiefe geneigt und nicht nivelliert, erschienen sie überproportional auf dem Feld. Sie flackerten, wie von einem sich noch kalibrierenden Hologrammprojektor über das Feld geworfen, waren nur für ein paar Sekunden stabil in ihrer Darstellung. Ihr Licht erreichte den Boden vor mir und brach sich in nervösen, forcierten Formen: verzerrte Trapeze, die für Momente zu Hohlzylindern wurden, Drachenvierecke, die durch die Äste der umstehenden Büsche in eine Aneinanderreihung schmaler Rauten geschnitten waren. Jede Form fand sich augenblicklich um ihre geometrische Reinheit betrogen. Polyeder oder Vielflächner, Drachenviereck – ein paar wenige dieser Bezeichnungen konnte ich noch aus der Schulzeit herüberretten. Sie waren für dieses Spiel gänzlich nutzlos. Sie wurden schneller, ich machte sie schneller, weil ich fähig sein wollte, »ohne Kenntnis, wie ein Blinder, dem man von Farben redet« (B.S.) zu begreifen, tappte damit jedoch nur zum wiederholten Male in die Falle. Die Beschleunigung verschmierte die Konturen der Formen, die nur mehr als transparente Wolke vor mir erschienen, welche sich nun bedrohlich anhob. Sie atmete wie eine Person, die künstlich mit Sauerstoff versorgt wird. Eine komplett von der Eigeninitiative unabhängige Lebenserhaltung, dachte ich, bedeutet doch, dass man ersetzt wurde. Tanz, Engelssprache, der Brunnen steigt und steigt, jetzt sollte die Gegenwart kommen, die sich, an den Marionettenfäden der Vergangenheit und Zukunft hängend, ohne Orientierung im Kreis dreht und bisher so elendig über den Boden schleppen musste.

Ich erinnerte mich an einen Nachmittag im Januar, an dem mir das erste Mal versprochen wurde, mein Wunsch könnte sich erfüllen. Auf meinem Bett liegend, nahm ich im Dämmerzustand mehrere tiefblaue Körper wahr, die mit einer Unmittelbarkeit sichtbar wurden, die mich

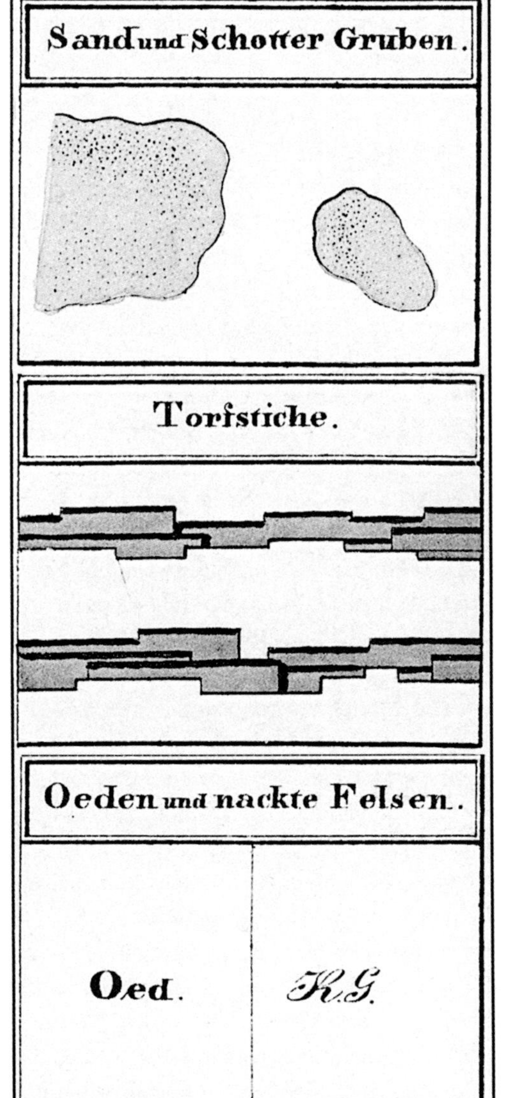
Sand und Schotter Gruben.
Torfstiche.
Oeden und nackte Felsen.
Oed.
K.G.

vermuten ließ, dass sie schon immer dort gewesen sind; verhangen nur von dem gleichen Licht, das die offensichtlichste Lüge noch anmutig wirken lässt. Es waren drei große, unregelmäßige Dreiecke, die versuchten, sich zusammenzufügen. Ihr Treiben war ruhig, fast zärtlich, obwohl die ungeraden Winkel verhinderten, dass sie zu einem Ganzen wurden. In stoischer Manier schoben sie sich auseinander, nur um es erneut zu versuchen. Jedes der Dreiecke hatte eine direkte Verbindung zu mir, zu einem Teil meiner Person. Mir wurde rasch klar, dass ihr Kern nicht in dem Drang lag, zu einem Ganzen zu werden, sondern in ihrer kontinuierlichen Bewegung, die keine Fragen stellte. Sie waren wie kleine Karten ohne jede Beschriftung, die sich nur durch ihre Beweglichkeit in einem begrenzten Bereich erklärten und mir unmissverständlich mitteilten, dass die Notwendigkeit, Bedeutungen durch Zeichen und Symbole zu fixieren, spätestens durch Buchstaben und die Wörter, die sie bilden, betrogen werden musste. Kindisch lachend, dachte ich an verstreute Aufzeichnungen, die eine Resilienz bewiesen, die mir stupide vorkam: *Hast du dir jemals das Maß aller Erlebnisse jedes einzelnen Menschen vorgestellt? Wären es nur endlose Variationen einer überschaubaren Anzahl an Themen? »Vom Absoluten reden ist das Bestreben der Larven« / das Zweifeln war nie meine Methode, sondern mein Ausgangspunkt / ich schärfe meine Sinne nicht für den Fortschritt, sondern für das Erkennen selbst kleinster Verletzungen / wäre ich clever, würde ich über meine Generation nachdenken / die Nabelschau muss sich, wenn sie durch Hass auf den Nabel geprägt ist und somit schon längst ihre Möglichkeiten ausgeschöpft hat, doch endlich auflösen.*

Der letzte Buchstabe wurde überflüssig, drehte sich nach einem Hammerschlag auf den Kopf und fiel nach kurzem Hin und Her mit dem Gewinsel eines bloßgestellten Schwindlers auf den Boden. Wasser aus unbekannter Quelle füllte das Zimmer, reinigte den Buchstaben von seinem Staub und trug ihn weg. Als ich begann zu sprechen, vernahm ich nur ein weiches Rauschen. Das Rauschen veränderte sich auch mit einem jähzornigen Schrei nicht, den ich ausstieß. Er war kein Ausdruck, bedeutete nichts mehr – keine Reaktion, keine Veränderung. Viel mehr glichen meine Worte einem Schrei in ihrer verfehlten Funktion, das Grundrauschen der Welt in erträgliche Laute zu stückeln. Mit den Knien eines Gläubigen, der sich durch die ausbleibende Antwort auf dem Höhepunkt seines Gebetes noch bestärkt sieht, versuchte ich mich in meine Unterlage zu graben und wieder einen Unterschied zu mir selbst zu spüren. Eine anonyme Leere war nicht, was ich hinter den Buchstaben vermutete.

Das Licht, das die Buchstaben abwarfen und jetzt in Formen auf dem Boden vor mir sichtbar war, ließ mir keinen anderen Weg, als erneut zu viel zu wollen. Dieses Mal gab ich dem Feld seine Buchstaben und den Formen ihre Namen, doch ich traute mir nicht. Auch zu diesem Zeitpunkt war ich noch von einer natürlichen, wenn auch verborgenen, Ordnung der Dinge überzeugt.

Contributors

Valeria Calderoni is a cinephile from the ceramics town of Red Desert. She studied Communication and International Relations in Bologna and works as digital analyst in Berlin.

Benedikt Eiden is a photo editor and publisher. He lives in Berlin roaming the past.

Rumen Lasev studies literature in Berlin. He is interested in the arcane, in old traditions and beliefs.

Christian Lenz is a film scholar, curator and librarian. He lives in Berlin.

Tim Nagel writes and makes music. He studies and works in Berlin.

Lisa Schug works in Berlin's independent archives and loves everything DIY. Her weakness is pastry.

Image Credits

p. 25: *The Dream Of Garuda* (*Karura No Yume*, 1994)
© Kokuei/Stance Company

p. 32-33: *Heaven's Story* (*Hasegawa & Nahana*, 2010)
© Freestone Productions/Stance Company

p. 46: from *L'alchimie et son livre muet* (1677), Isaac Baulot

p. 72: Inge Müller
© Akademie der Künste, Berlin, Inge-Müller-Archiv, Nr. 501-002

p. 77: Inge Müller
© Akademie der Künste, Berlin, Inge-Müller-Archiv, Nr. 501-012

p. 86-87: Aufnahmen der ehemaligen alten Abdeckerei
© Akademie der Künste, Berlin, Wolfgang-Hilbig-Archiv, Nr. 736-010/012

p. 93: Wolfgang Hilbig
© Akademie der Künste, Berlin, Wolfgang-Hilbig-Archiv, Nr. 768

p. 105: Vox Populi! live in Paris (1987)
© Françoise Girard

p. 113: "Und wenn sie nicht gestorben sind" by Unica Zürn
© Brinkmann & Bose

p. 135: Legende zu den Kartenblättern des Franziszeischen Katasters (1824)

Index

Acknowledgements & Hails

A huge thank you goes to all the contributors! This issue obviously wouldn't have been possible without your help. Further thanks also go to Christl Schönheit, Axel Kyrou & Mitra Kyrou-Khalatbari, Susan Stock, Sarah B. Bolen, Eleni Efthimiou, Alfred Hilsberg, Peter Weiss, Richard H. Kirk, H. & E., Zabriskie Buchladen, Antenne Books, HHV and last but not least the NASA for their incredible photo archives.

We'll meet again.

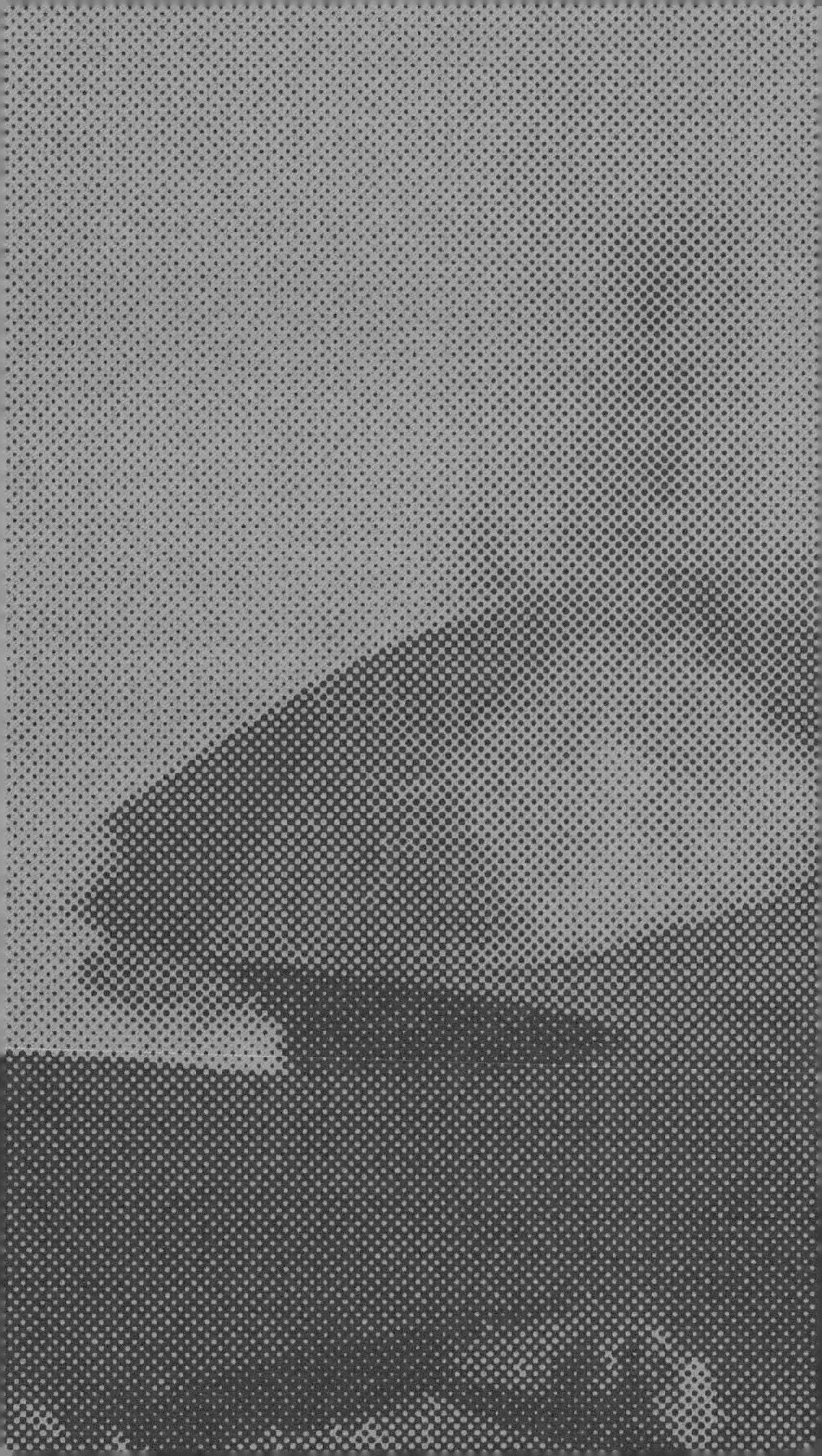